MAC address OUI's on .... page 10

D1278914

DHCP

A Guide to Dynamic TCP/IP Network Configuration

ISBN 0-13-099721-8

9 780130 997210

90000

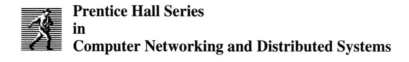

**Prentice Hall Series
in
Computer Networking and Distributed Systems**

Radia Perlman, Series Editor

DHCP

A Guide to Dynamic TCP/IP Network Configuration

Berry Kercheval

Prentice Hall PTR
Upper Saddle River, NJ 07458
http://www.phptr.com

Editorial/production supervision: *Joan L. McNamara*
Cover design director: *Jerry Votta*
Cover designer: *Anthony Gemmellaro*
Manufacturing manager: *Alexis R. Heydt*
Marketing manager: *Miles Williams*
Acquisitions editor: *Mary Franz*
Editorial assistant: *Noreen Regina*

©1999 by Prentice Hall PTR
Prentice-Hall, Inc.
A Simon & Schuster Company
Upper Saddle River, NJ 07458

Prentice Hall books are widely used by corporations and government agencies
for training, marketing, and resale.

The publisher offers discounts on this book when ordered in bulk quantities.
For more information, contact: Corporate Sales Department, Phone: 800-382-3419;
Fax: 201-236-7141; E-mail: corpsales@prenhall.com; or write: Prentice Hall PTR,
Corp. Sales Dept., One Lake Street, Upper Saddle River, NJ 07458.

Printed in the United States of America
10 9 8 7 6 5 4 3 2 1

ISBN   0-13-099721-8

Prentice-Hall International (UK) Limited, *London*
Prentice-Hall of Australia Pty. Limited, *Sydney*
Prentice-Hall Canada Inc., *Toronto*
Prentice-Hall Hispanoamericana, S.A., *Mexico*
Prentice-Hall of India Private Limited, *New Delhi*
Prentice-Hall of Japan, Inc., *Tokyo*
Simon & Schuster Asia Pte. Ltd., *Singapore*
Editora Prentice-Hall do Brasil, Ltda., *Rio de Janeiro*

I dedicated my first book to my wife,
and on reflection
she is still the most important person in my life,
so this book is also dedicated to my wife Alene,
with all my love.

Contents

Preface

This book explains the Dynamic Host Configuration Protocol (DHCP). DHCP allows computers to be configured, in the best case, by merely plugging them in and turning them on. At the appropriate point in the boot sequence, the newly connected computer will search for a DHCP server and negotiate with it for an IP address and other configuration parameters such as DNS server addresses, default routers, and a host of other parameters.

How all this works is the subject of this book.

After a high-level introduction, we'll take a look at the BOOTP protocol in Chapter 2, which is the foundation on which DHCP was built.

The DHCP protocol itself is described in Chapter 3, followed by a detailed look at operations from the client and server points of view in Chapters 4 and 5, respectively.

Chapter 6 discusses the relay agents that allow one DHCP server to manage addresses on more than one subnet at a time, and Chapter 7 describes how DHCP can update DNS with correct information as it hands out addresses.

Chapter 8 describes the administration side of DHCP, with some detail about popular servers.

The rest of the book is oriented toward the future. Chapter 9 is about the forthcoming integration of DHCP with directory services, specifically LDAP, and Chapter 10 is about the new version of DHCP that will support IPv6.

Chapter 11 finishes off with a look at what's going on in the IETF working group.

An appendix on DHCP software and one with the principal RFCs describing the protocol wraps up the book, along with a glossary and index.

Note on Language

You will notice that terms like "BOOTP" include the term "protocol" as the "P", yet the usage "BOOTP protocol" is frequent. To a language purist, this can be as annoying as "ATM Machine" or "PIN Number". I beg your indulgence with the explanation that in this book, and indeed in the networking community, terms like "BOOTP" or "DHCP" have come to mean more than just the protocols. They include systems, programs, databases, back-ends, front-ends, user interfaces—in short, the entire system. When I wish to refer specifically to the protocol aspect of, say, DHCP, I will say "DHCP protocol".

In addition, I've tried to be gender-neutral, but probably haven't completely succeeded; I have no wish to offend anyone and hope this advance apology will suffice if I inadvertently do.

Internet Draft Notice

Sometimes I refer to Internet Drafts which are both the most current source of Internet information and the most unstable. Here is the warning attached to every Internet Draft:

> Internet-Drafts are working documents of the Internet Engineering Task Force (IETF), its areas, and its working groups. Note that other groups may also distribute working documents as Internet-Drafts.
>
> Internet-Drafts are draft documents valid for a maximum of six months and may be updated, replaced, or obsoleted by other documents at any time. It is inappropriate to use Internet-Drafts as reference material or to cite them other than as "work in progress."
>
> To learn the current status of any Internet-Draft, please check the "1id-abstracts.txt" listing contained in the Internet-Drafts Shadow Directories on ftp.is.co.za (Africa), nic.nordu.net (Europe), munnari.oz.au (Pacific Rim), ds.internic.net (US East Coast), or ftp.isi.edu (US West Coast).

Acknowledgments

I would like to thank the reviewers who helped me make fewer egregious errors in this book than I might otherwise have committed: Tom Limoncelli, Santosh Shanbhag, Markus Gutschke, and Jon Finke.

Jim Chavis of Intuit graciously allowed me to abuse one of his Windows NT servers to get the screen shots in Chapter 8.

Series editor Radia Perlman deserves credit for reviewing, as well as talking me into writing the book.

At Prentice Hall, Mary Franz and Noreen Regina are a great team that keeps track of all the things to do to get a book published *besides* just writing it.

Finally, I'd like to give special thanks to my wife, Alene, for her great patience and encouragement while this book was being written.

Introduction

Say first, of God above or man below,
What can we reason but from what we know?
Alexander Pope, *Essay on Man*

The dynamic configuration of computers is a topic of much interest these days, as computer networks become larger and more complex. The complex issues involved can daunt anyone. I hope in this book to give a basic knowledge from which you can, like Pope, reason to the solutions of your problems.

Network administrators may wish to control the parameters assigned to computers based on the type of computer, the segment of the local network to which the computer is attached, which user is logging in, or in accordance with local policies that must be enforced. The parameters to be assigned to a computer can be many and varied. From the simple assignment of an IP address, to telling the computer its default routers, name servers, file servers and more, flexibility is demanded by today's sophisticated networks.

The ideal is to deliver this information without requiring harried administrators to hand-configure every computer in the company, as well as relieving them of the need to track down and admonish the pesky users that insist on reconfiguring their own systems. How can we do this? One answer is the Dynamic Host Configuration Protocol (DHCP), which is an open standard promulgated by the Internet Engineering Task Force (IETF) to provide configuration parameters to Internet hosts.

This book explains DHCP, both in broad strokes and in detail. It should be useful to anyone wishing to understand, configure, use, or implement DHCP, such as:

- System administrators wanting to understand DHCP so as to configure their networks and ease their management burden.
- Network managers wishing to understand the technical issues involved.
- Network programmers wanting to interoperate with existing implementations.
- Computer users wanting to know what's going on under the covers and why they keep getting a different IP address.

1.1   Overview of DHCP and Related Protocols

First, to whet your appetite, here's a quick overview of protocols. If you find terms that are unfamiliar, check out the digression on terminology later in this chapter, or the glossary in the back.

First came the Bootstrap Protocol (BOOTP, Chapter 2). BOOTP allows a computer to broadcast a message to a server, asking for basic parameters: its IP address and the name of a file to load. It is a request/response protocol: The client sends a request out with its Ethernet address, saying to the world, or at least to the local network, "Here I am! Boot me!".

If a BOOTP server is around, listening for just such messages, it will hear the cry and look up in its files to see what kind of configuration the network manager has decreed shall be sent to this client. If it finds something, the information gets packaged up into a response that gets sent back to the Ethernet address of the client. (The client may be unaware of its IP address at this point.)

If a BOOTP client is on a different subnet from the server, a relay agent (Chapter 6) can be employed to forward messages from the client to the server and back. This is not quite as simple as it sounds; the relay agent must know where the server really is, since just rebroadcasting on the new network is not very friendly. A power failure that causes all the machines in an organization to reboot at once leads to a big pileup at the BOOTP server; making all these packets broadcast just makes things worse because all the other machines on the subnet have to process and discard the packets.

The Dynamic Host Configuration Protocol (DHCP, Chapter 3) is, technically, an extension to BOOTP. Using BOOTP, a computer broadcasts a request for basic parameters: its IP address and the name of the file to load. Trying to fit DHCP's additional parameters led to some interesting contortions to fit the data into the packet.

Two major differences between the two protocols are: first, DHCP dynamically assigns an IP address to a client; and second, there is a mechanism for adding optional information to messages; indeed, some of the core DHCP information is carried in "options". This makes adding a new option easier, since a protocol redesign is not necessary.

The DHCP protocol is also a request/response protocol, but in two stages. First, the client trying to boot sends out a Discover message, fishing for DHCP servers. The servers that take the bait reply with Offer messages, in which they indicate the configuration they would give the client if they win. The client looks over the offers, picks one, and sends a Request message to formalize the arrangement. Finally, the server sends an ACK to acknowledge that it got the request, the parameters are locked in, and the client can go ahead and use them.

1.2 The IETF and Relevant Documents

DHCP and its related protocols like BOOTP are standards developed by the Internet Engineering Task Force (IETF). The IETF is an organization made up of, well, anyone who cares to join. The IETF is divided into *working groups* that are formed for a given task. DHCP development is overseen by the *Dynamic Host Configuration* working group.

The main output of a working group, besides heat and noise, is documents. They are made as follows: In a meeting of the working group, or in a discussion on the associated mailing list, it is decided that a given document is needed to describe, say, DHCP Options for Self-configuring Internet Toasters. Someone, often an engineer employed by a toaster manufacturer, will volunteer to produce a draft of the document. This is called an *Internet Draft*, and it is made widely available on the IETF ftp site and its mirrors.

Next, people in the working group (and anyone else interested) read the document and discuss it. Perhaps a frustrated toaster user will propose modifications that will make it easier to configure Internet toasters. Rival toaster manufacturers will propose changes that make their toasters work at least as well. This will then become a revised draft.

Eventually, the working group will come to a rough consensus that the document is ready, and it will be promoted out of the working group as a proposed standard, which for historic reasons is called a "Request for Comments," or *RFC*. After some implementation experience, it may move to full standard status and vendors can proudly ship standards-based Internet toasters with confidence that they will all work happily together.

DHCP is such an IETF standard. RFC 2131 is called "Dynamic Host Configuration Protocol" and it defines the current version of DHCP. It also obsoletes RFC 1541, an earlier version of DHCP.

Now, "obsolete" doesn't mean a document can be thrown away. Obsolete RFCs are kept for historical reasons, and in some cases, as references. For example, RFC 1533 officially RFC obsoletes 1497, yet refers to it for the format of the extensions.

The principal, current RFCs relevant to DHCP can be found in Appendix C, and on-line from any number of sources. They can always be found on the IETF Web site, `http://www.ietf.org`.

Here's a list of all the relevant DHCP RFCs:

- RFC 783 "The TFTP Protocol".
- RFC 951 "BOOTSTRAP PROTOCOL" (updated by 1532).
- RFC 1048 "BOOTP Vendor Information Extensions" (obsoleted by 1084).
- RFC 1084 "BOOTP Vendor Information Extensions" (obsoleted by 1395).

- RFC 1395 "BOOTP Vendor Information Extensions" (obsoleted by 1497).
- RFC 1497 "BOOTP Vendor Information Extensions" (obsoleted by 1533).
- RFC 1532 "Clarifications and Extensions for the Bootstrap Protocol" (obsoleted by 1542).
- RFC 1533 "DHCP Options and BOOTP Vendor Extensions".
- RFC 1534 "Interoperation Between DHCP and BOOTP".
- RFC 1542 "Clarifications and Extensions for the Bootstrap Protocol".
- RFC 2131 "Dynamic Host Configuration Protocol".
- RFC 2132 "DHCP Options and BOOTP Vendor Extensions".
- RFC 2241 "DHCP Options for Novell Directory Services".

1.3   A Digression on Terminology

Many authors writing technical books just dive in and assume that you know what they're talking about. I'm going to do that too; but first, here's a safe place to get your toes wet and adjust to the water temperature before taking the plunge.

Below are some terms that are used throughout this book. A more complete list can be found in the Glossary.

network. This is an unfortunately fuzzy term. I mean it to be the transmission medium over which computers exchange data, together with the equipment that facilitates the exchange. This includes network cables, hubs, routers, modems, switches, and, well, anything that's not an end-user's computer.

subnet. A subnet is a portion of a network with a contiguous range of IP addresses. It is usually a portion of a larger address allocation, and is defined by a network address and a subnet mask. It is often associated with a network segment.

octet. An octet is a byte, these days. Some older computers used storage units that were not multiples of eight bits; PDP-10s, one of the computers on the ARPANET in the early days (and in some ways still one of the better-designed machines and operating systems around), had 36-bit words, with four nine-bit bytes in each word. To avoid confusion, pioneer network researchers coined the term *octet* to mean eight bits of data, regardless of the fundamental size of a given machine's storage.

packet. A packet is a unit of computer data that can be sent from one computer to another over a network. Packets are usually encapsulated, or wrapped up in network frames that are transmitted on the physical network medium.

datagram. This is a packet that contains within itself enough information for the network to deliver it to its destination. Typically Internet packets contain both the source and destination IP addresses. This is in contrast to connection-oriented networks, like Asynchronous Transfer Mode (ATM) or the phone system, where packets contain only enough information to identify the connection they should travel over, and the routing to the destination is maintained inside the network.

host. A host is a computer attached to a network.

server. A server is a computer attached to a network (therefore it's also a host) that provides a service for other computers on the network. A server can also be the program or process on a given computer that implements the service. Examples of servers include mail servers, which receive and store your mail until you are ready to read it, and Web servers that provide World Wide Web pages to Internet surfers on demand.

client. A client is a computer attached to a network that uses a service. It can also be a program or process on a computer that implements the client half of a client/server protocol. A Web browser like Netscape or Internet Explorer is a good example of a client. Note, however, that a given computer can be a client and a server *at the same time*. The computer I'm typing this book on, for example, not only runs my Web browser, but also runs the Web server for my domain, kerch.com.

Internet. The concatenation of networks that spans the planet and brings people from all over the world together on the Web, in email, and in countless other ways.

network segment. A piece of a network, usually not including any equipment that connects it to another piece of network. A single section of an Ethernet, for instance, or one token ring. Also called a LAN segment. It is often associated with a subnet.

router. A machine that forwards packets from one network segment to another. A typical router will receive network frames on one network interface, extract the packet, decide where it should go, wrap it up in the appropriate frame for the new network, and transmit it.

gateway. Another, older term for router.

bridge. A bridge is a machine that connects two network segments together without doing routing: The original, most simple bridges would merely transmit on one interface all the frames received on all other interfaces. Bridges quickly became rather more smart than this; they can, for instance, "learn" which destination addresses "live" on the segments connected to their various interfaces, and only transmit frames to the segment on which their destination lies.

IP. The Internet protocol; the basic protocol of the Internet which allows hosts connected to the Internet to exchange packets.

IP address. The 32-bit address of a host connected to the Internet. Must be globally unique.[1]

---

[1] Enterprise networks that are not connected to the global Internet, or that use special proxy or address translation systems, may have addresses that are replicated in other non-connected networks. In general, within a single Internet (global or corporate), unique addresses must be used so that routing will work properly.

port. A 16-bit number that is used to identify the program or entity on a computer that produced or will consume a packet. A port allows a computer to provide multiple services or host multiple clients.

Ethernet. A network technology in wide use as a Local Area Network (LAN), invented at Xerox PARC. Ethernet hosts transmit whenever they feel like it, but can detect "collisions" when two transmit at the same time, and can back off and try again. Ethernet has its own address scheme that is different from IP addresses.

ARP. When a computer wants to send a packet on an Ethernet, it sends it using source and destination Ethernet addresses. If all it has is the IP address of the destination, how can it learn the Ethernet address? The Address Resolution Protocol (ARP) provides a means for doing this. Put simply, the computer broadcasts a message asking "Yo, who is IP address X?" and the computer whose IP address is X replies, "Hey, that's me, my Ethernet address is Y".

1.4 Finite State Machines

Computer scientists have a useful tool called a finite state machine, which has many interesting mathematical properties and can be used to model computation and to reason about it. A simplified finite state machine is often used as a tool for computer networking to describe protocols. I'll explain this simple usage here, without most of the mathematics. The DHCP protocol is also described as a finite state machine, so a few minutes spent perusing this section now may pay off when you get to Chapter 3.

The basic idea is simple. Imagine that you are looking for a job. You could be said to be in the state "unemployed". If you apply for work at a company, you can move to the state "applied". If the company rejects you, you go back to "unemployed"; if the company accepts you, you go to the state "hired-waiting". This means that you are hired, but haven't actually started working.

On your first day of work, you move to "hired-orienting". You are filling out paperwork, signing up for health benefits, and (in the US) proving that you are allowed to work; that is, you are not an illegal alien. If you can't provide proof that you can work, you go back to "unemployed".

After all hurdles are passed, you are "working", a state in which most people hope to stay a long time.

Now, notice that each state has several attributes:

- Each state has a name.
- Each state has a set of transitions that take you to other states.
- Each transition is associated with an event.

So, our hypothetical job hunt can be summarized as in Table 1-1. When implementing this state machine, when an event occurs, we remember our current state, look in the table for the row with the current state and current event, and choose our new state from the row. In some cases, there will be an action to perform that is associated with the move to the new state; for example, if you are fired and move to the "unemployed" state, an action associated with that transition might be "file for unemployment insurance".

Table 1-1 Job Search State Table

State Name	Event	New State
unemployed	submit application	applied
applied	rejected	unemployed
applied	accepted	hired-waiting
hired-waiting	time to start	hired-orienting
hired-waiting	change mind	unemployed
hired-orienting	fill out papers	working
hired-orienting	illegal alien	unemployed
working	fired	unemployed
working	quit	unemployed

State machines can also be represented as diagrams. For example, Table 1-1 is shown as a diagram in Figure 1-1. Here, each state is represented with a circle, and each possible transition is shown as an arrow. Usually the arrows are labeled with the transition events and actions, as in Figure 3-3; but for simplicity, this figure omits them.

It should be clear that when a protocol is presented in this way, it is possible to identify possible problems: States with no transitions to a corresponding new state are obvious, and events that try to cause two different transitions become apparent.

These diagrams and tables not only clarify how a protocol is designed and makes "correctness" or missing cases easier to see, they make implementation straightforward. For example, if we were coding the job search example in C, we might write some code like that shown below. Observe how each row of the table has a case in the switch: If we're in state X, then we do the X actions; change the state, and go around the loop again.

While coding the example, I got to the part below marked "oops" and realized that in the "applied" state, there is no specification of what to do if neither event happens—what happens if we are neither accepted nor rejected? I thought about going back and fixing it, but decided to leave it as an example of how this design and implementation technique can lead to the discovery of left-out situations.

Often the solution in such cases is to merely stay in the same state until one of the triggering events occurs; this is represented on diagrams as an arrow that loops back to the same state, and in code it's often just falling to the bottom

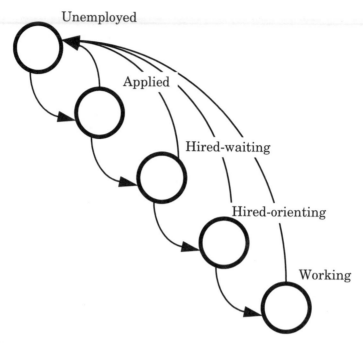

Figure 1-1 Job Search State Machine Diagram

of the loop for another try. Practical implementations, of course, will do some type of trick to suspend or block until an interesting event happens, so that the protocol code doesn't spin endlessly checking for infrequent events and so the computer can be used for other things.

Here is a sample of how code for the job search state machine might be written, in a C-like language:

```
while(not_retired) {
    switch(state) {
        case UNEMPLOYED:
            submit_application; state = APPLIED; break;
        case APPLIED:
            if(rejected) {
                state = UNEMPLOYED; break;
            }
            else if(accepted) {
                state = HIRED_WAITING; break;
            }
            else ???; /* oops */
        .... /* some code omitted... */
        case WORKING:
            if(fired || quit) state = UNEMPLOYED; break;
    }
}
```

1.5   Byte Order and Network Transmissions

The majority of computers in use today use eight-bit units of storage called *bytes*. Most network interfaces transmit data a byte at a time. The transmission of a larger unit of data, such as, say, a 16-bit port number, causes a small problem. Since the port number takes up two bytes, which byte do we send first? One obvious answer is to observe that since each byte of storage has its own address, store the port number into memory, and send the bytes in the order in which they are stored in memory: the byte with the lower address first, and the byte with the higher address second.

The problem here is that not all computers store the bytes into memory in the same order! This is typically a characteristic of the computer's processor. For instance, Intel processors tend to operate differently than Motorola processors. And, when we look at four- or eight-byte numbers, the problem can get even worse.

To get around this, the Internet protocols specify a "network byte order": the order in which bytes must get transmitted so as to be properly interpreted by the receiving computer. In network code, one often sees calls to functions with names like `ntohs()` and `htons()`; these stand for "network to host, short" and "host to network - short". These functions convert from network byte order to host byte order and back. Similar functions are defined for other sizes of numbers as well.

Why should we care? It turns out that because of the special needs of the protocol, many DHCP implementations build packets "by hand", in local buffers, rather than relying on the operating system to build packets with their data. When doing this, one needs to be aware of the network byte order problem. If you ever do some network programming and discover that your program works fine with, say, Sun SparcStations, but fails miserably with Pentium-based Linux machines, look for a byte ordering problem.

1.6   Classes and Subnets

IP addresses are, in the current version, 32 bits or four bytes long.[2] These are divided into classes according to the value of the first byte.

If the first byte is between one and 127 (i.e., the highest order bit is a zero), the network is called Class A, and can contain 16,777,216 (2^{24}) addresses in the remaining 24 bits. The first byte's value, between one and 127, is called the network number, and the remaining 24 bits are called the host number.

If the first byte is between 128 and 191, (highest order two bits are '10'), the network is Class B. The second byte is part of the network number, and the host part can have 65,536 (2^{16}) addresses.

---

[2] IP Version Six (IPv6) expands this to 128 bits; see Chapter 10 titled "IP Version 6 and DHCP" for more information.

If the first byte is between 192 and 223 (high three bits are '110'), the network is Class C. The second and third bytes of the address are the network number, and 256 hosts can be addressed with the eight-bit host part.

Addresses with an initial byte between 224 and 239 (highest four bits are '1110') are Class D addresses reserved for multicast. Class E and higher are "reserved for further study".

In some cases, a larger network may be split into pieces; this is called *subnetting*. It is often done so that routing internal to the network can be done efficiently; for example, a Class A network 10.0.0.0 might assign all hosts on Ethernet segment 1 addresses like 10.0.X.X, and all hosts on segment 2 addresses like 10.80.X.X. This allows the router between the segments to do a simple masking of the destination addresses of each packet to decide which network segment to send them to.

A relatively new technology, Classless Interdomain Routing (CIDR), makes a lot of this discussion moot. CIDR networks are just a network address and a subnet mask of however many bits are significant. A full class A address like 10.0.0.0 becomes 10.0.0.0/8, with the '8' indicating that the first 8 bits (the host number in traditional "classful" terms) is the network part and the rest is the host part.

A Class C like 192.168.123.0 would be 192.168.1.0/24, but if the network manager wished to divide it into two equal subnets, he could do it with 192.168.1.0/25 and 192.168.1.128/25.

The *cool* part, though, is that the same technique allows you to aggregate networks into bigger nets: 192.168.0.0 and 192.168.1.0 could be combined into 192.168.0.0/23, for instance. This allows routing tables to be smaller, forestalling the day when the net collapses. IPv6 (Chapter 10) is intended to deal with this, but as yet does not enjoy widespread deployment.

1.7 The Example Network

Figure 1-2 illustrates a diagram of a sample network. I won't call it a "typical" network because it has been artificially configured to illustrate the points in the book, not to illustrate "best practice". This diagram will be used throughout the book as a fixed reference point to minimize confusion and present alternative configurations.

The IP addresses used in the sample network are drawn from the Class A network 10, which is one of the networks reserved in RFC1597 for private networks. Thus, these addresses are unlikely to match any "real" hosts on the Internet.

The MAC (or "Ethernet") addresses all have the same first three bytes: 01:23:45. This part of an Ethernet address is called the Organizationally Unique Identifier, or OUI, and identifies the company or other organization that built the hardware involved. For example, all Ethernet devices built by Xerox have the OUI 00:00:AA, while those built by Sun Microsystems have an OUI of 80:00:20. These numbers are assigned by the IEEE, and a list can be found on-line at

http://standards.ieee.org/regauth/oui/index.html.

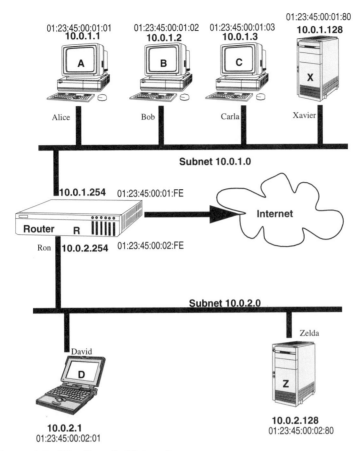

Figure 1-2 The Sample Network

The OUI used in the sample network is not reserved for any company, at least as of the writing of this book. Further, when domain names are used, they are all given as belonging to "`domain.com`", which is a domain name reserved for examples.

So, the addresses and hostnames used in this book are intended to be completely fictitious. Don't try to ping them, connect to them, or log in to them; it won't work.

Hostnames given in URLs, or instructions for fetching RFCs and the like are, of course, real, or at least as real as I could make them at the time this book went to press.

Getting back to the network as shown, we see that it has two network segments connected by a router R. The upper segment can be called the 10.0.1.0 network, and the lower segment the 10.0.2.0 network. The subnet mask for each is 255.255.255.0.

Connected to the 10.0.1.0 network are three clients named A, B, and C, one server named X, and the router R interface with address 10.0.1.254.

The 10.0.2.0 network has one client named D, server Z, and the router R interface with address 10.0.2.254.

Obviously, packets from host A for server Z have to pass through router R.

1.8 Plan for the Rest of the Book

The rest of this book is laid out as follows:
>BOOTP, The Bootstrap Protocol
>The DHCP Protocol
>DHCP Operations: The Client's View
>DHCP Operations: The Server's View
>DHCP Relay Agents
>Dynamic DNS
>Administering DHCP
>Lightweight Directory Access Protocol and DHCP
>IP Version 6 and DHCP
>The Future of DHCP
>Appendix A: DHCP Vendors
>Appendix B: The Requests For Comment
>Appendix C: DHCP Software
>Glossary
>Index

BOOTP, The Bootstrap Protocol

Client and Server: Who Does What When?

The BOOTP Database

Protocol Basics

Routers and BOOTP

The Bootstrap Protocol (BOOTP) was developed to allow computers to initialize themselves over a network [RFC951]. It is limited compared to DHCP, but since DHCP was built on top of BOOTP, it is important to understand BOOTP's message structure and protocol before looking at DHCP proper.

Furthermore, since most DHCP implementations also function as BOOTP servers, if you are implementing DHCP, you'll most likely have to understand BOOTP anyway.

The usual BOOTP scenario involves a computer asking for information with which to initialize itself. It can ask a server for three pieces of information. First, it can get its IP address. This is, of course, useful so that it can initialize its network interface. Second, it can ask for the IP address of a machine called a "bootserver", which will supply a file for the machine to load and run. Third, it can get the name of the file it should load.

Armed with this information, the client can now initialize its network, connect to the bootserver (whose address it now knows), and load its assigned bootfile using a simple protocol like TFTP.

The bootfile will generally contain all the rest of the information the client needs for configuration, in a format that has significance only to the client. Indeed, the bootfile may be an entire software image that the client will load and run.

2.1   Client and Server: Who Does What When?

In BOOTP language, a "client" is a computer that is attempting to initialize itself, and a "server" is a computer that provides the initialization service. Typically, the client will be a PC or workstation attempting to boot, and the server will be, well, a server maintained by the organization that runs the local network.

BOOTP is based on UDP, so it is not a "reliable" protocol in the sense that there are no hard guarantees made by the protocol that a message sent from a client will ever arrive at the server, or vice versa. In practice, since BOOTP usually operates over local network segments, it turns out to be reliable in the sense that it usually works just fine.

There is no acknowledgment of the receipt of a UDP datagram sent back to the sender—that is, the sender of a UDP datagram cannot know whether the datagram was received by the destination, received and ignored, or lost in the network. Thus, a BOOTP client cannot know if its packet arrived successfully until a reply from the BOOTP server comes back.

To prevent clients from hanging in the "waiting for reply from the server" state forever if the initial packet is lost, clients using BOOTP will only wait for a certain amount of time before *assuming* that their packet was lost, and then send it again.

The BOOTP RFC does not mandate a particular retransmission strategy, but suggests one similar to the Ethernet exponential backoff [Metcalf and Boggs] used to retransmit Ethernet frames after collisions. This will tend to smooth out the flow of packets to the poor, overworked server trying to cope with hundreds of clients booting all at once, and is discussed below.

2.2   The BOOTP Database

A BOOTP server must keep a database of its clients, mapping each client's hardware address to its IP address and the specific bootfile that the client should be sent. This database need not be a full-blown relational database, of course; any scheme for keeping this information will suffice as long as the performance continues to be acceptable.

Two types of databases should be kept. The first one should be a list of IP addresses, indexed by the MAC address. When the server gets a BOOTP request from a client, it can use the MAC address in the packet to look up the correct IP address assigned to that client.

This database must be set up beforehand by the network manager, which can be tedious for a large installation—and incidentally explains some of the motivation for DHCP.

The other database takes the client's address and the string in the 'file' field and maps it to the name of the file the client should load and the address of the server to load it from. This too must be set up by the network manager before operations begin, or at least before a client can expect to be served.

2.3 Protocol Basics

The BOOTP protocol consists of a single packet exchange. First the client sends a BOOTREQUEST packet to the server, requesting that the server supply it with some information. Next, the server sends back a BOOTREPLY packet with the requested information. What could be simpler?

The details are a little more complex, of course.

2.3.1 Packet Format

Figure 2-1 shows the format of a BOOTP packet. The fields in the packet are as shown below (we follow the names used in the RFC):

op	One byte	This is the "op code" for the packet, indicating the packet type. If this field contains a value of one, it's a BOOTREQUEST packet; if it has a two, it's a BOOTREPLY; if it's some other value, it's something else—not a BOOTP packet at all. (We'll see some more values later on when we discover how DHCP is related to BOOTP.)
htype	One byte	This tells what type of hardware or MAC address is being used by the client. The codes are the same as used in the ARP protocol. A value of one means Ethernet, four means token ring, and so on.
hlen	One byte	The length of the hardware address, in bytes. Ethernet addresses are six bytes; ATM addresses are 20.
hops	One byte	Set to zero by the client; used in trans-router booting.
xid	4 bytes	The transaction ID is a random number chosen by the client. The server copies this ID into the reply message so that the client can match up replies it gets with requests that were sent.
secs	2 bytes	The number of seconds since the client started trying to boot.
Flags	2 bytes	These bytes contain 16 one-bit flags. The most significant bit is the Broadcast flag, discussed below. This field was unused until RFC1542 was published; it was just padding added to make sure that the next field, an IP address, started on a quad-word boundary. The RFC1542 authors decided the bytes could be useful after all. Unused flag bits must be set to zero.
ciaddr	4 bytes	Client IP address. If the booting client knows its IP address, it fills it in here. If not, it is set to zero.
yiaddr	4 bytes	"Your" IP address. If the ciaddr field was set to

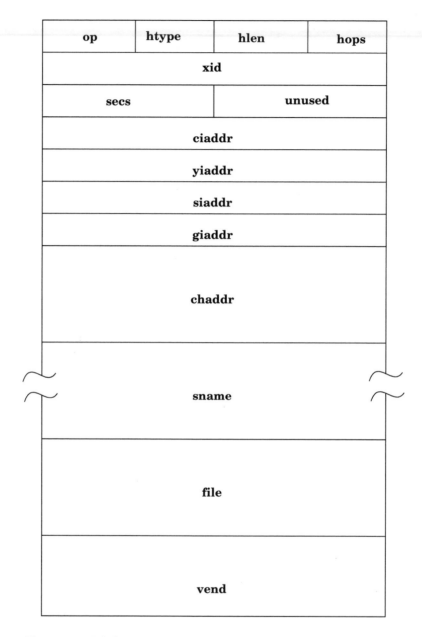

Figure 2-1 BOOTP Packet Format

		zero by the client, the server will choose an IP address for the client and fill it in here.	
siaddr	4 bytes	Server IP address. This is the IP address of the server that generated the reply.	
giaddr	4 bytes	Gateway address used in trans-router booting.	

`chaddr`	16 bytes	Client hardware address. The client here fills in its Ethernet or other MAC address, using up `hlen` bytes of this field.
`sname`	64 bytes	Server hostname, represented as a null-terminated string.
`file`	128 bytes	This is the name of the bootfile that the client should load and run.
`vend`	64 bytes	This area can be used for various vendor-specific extensions.

2.3.2 Sending the Request

To begin the BOOTP exchange, the client machine must create and send a BOOTREQUEST packet. This packet must be formatted as follows.

2.3.2.1 IP Packet Setup

If the address of the server is known, then the destination address of the IP packet is set to it; otherwise, the destination can be set to the broadcast address (255.255.255.255). If the client knows its own IP address, then that is set as the IP source address; otherwise, it can be set to zero (0.0.0.0).

Since BOOTP uses UDP packets, the client must build a UDP header as well. The important fields in the UDP header are packet length, set to the length of the packet; source port, set to 'BOOTP client' (68); and destination port, set to 'BOOTP server' (67).[1]

The UDP checksum is optional, but strongly recommended, especially here. An undetected corrupted BOOTP packet could ruin a client's whole day.

Note that the client can still initiate a BOOTP protocol exchange even if it knows nothing about the network at all! Even without knowing the local network address or subnet mask, any client can still send a broadcast packet.

2.3.2.2 Filling in the BOOTREQUEST Packet

Let's watch a client in our sample network attempt to initialize itself using BOOTP. Client A is going to try to boot from server X. Further, let's assume that client A doesn't know its own IP address yet.

Since the client is going to send a BOOTREQUEST, the `op` field should be filled in with the code for BOOTREQUEST, that is, 1.

The client IP address field (`ciaddr`) is set to the same thing as the IP source address in the packet header: the client's IP address, if known, or 0.0.0.0.

The hardware address part is filled in appropriately: `htype` is set to the correct hardware address type (as defined in the "Assigned Numbers" RFC, again) and `hlen` is set to the length of the hardware address. For Ethernet,

---

[1] The BOOTP port numbers are defined in the "Assigned Numbers" RFC, issued periodically. At the time of writing this book, RFC1700 was the latest version.

`htype` should be set to 1 and `hlen` to 6. The `chaddr` field should be filled in with the hardware address: the Ethernet address from the Ethernet adapter (if the client is using Ethernet, of course). The `chaddr` field is 16 bytes long, while the Ethernet address is 6 bytes long. The remaining bytes should be set to zeros.[2]

The transaction ID, `xid`, is just set to a 'random' number, and `secs` is set to the number of seconds since the client started trying to boot. Some servers may give some kind of preference to clients that have been trying to boot for a long time, but this is easily abused by unscrupulous clients setting it to a large value to get preferential treatment, so some servers ignore the field.

The server name field, `sname`, can be used for the name of the server from which this client wants to boot; this can be useful if the name is known but the IP address is not.

The `file` field can contain a "generic" bootfile name (the BOOTP RFC gives "unix" and "ethertip" as examples). This can be a hint to the server about what kind of bootfile the client would like to get back.

The `vend` field is used for vendor-specific information. It is recommended that a unique, four-byte "Magic Number" be used to identify the vendor involved, and thus the type of information that is placed here.

Figure 2-2 shows the filled-in BOOTREQUEST packet, ready to be transmitted from A to X.

2.3.2.3 Sending the BOOTREQUEST Packet

Now the client has a filled-in BOOTREQUEST that it is ready to send. The IP destination address is either the broadcast address (255.255.255.255) or the address of the BOOTP server it wishes to talk to. All the fields appropriate to this request have been filled in, the UDP checksum has been calculated, and it's ready to go.

Now, if the destination is the broadcast address, the client can just send it off, and the lower level network driver can send it using the broadcast hardware address.

Having sent the BOOTREQUEST packet, the client waits for a reply. In some cases, for whatever reason, the expected reply may not come back. The server could be down. The server could decide not to respond to the client. The network cable between the two computers could be unplugged, or cut by a backhoe, or a comet could fall on the computer room, or...well, anything.

What to do in this case? Well, since most of the time the problem will most likely *not* be a rogue asteroid, but something that will be fixed shortly, it's a good idea to just try again. But it's not a good idea to try again after a fixed timeout. Imagine, say, a power failure in a large office for an insurance company's claims department with a thousand computers for the claims examiners. After the

---

[2] Indeed, the authors of the BOOTP RFC suggest setting the *entire* packet to zeros before beginning to fill it in. This tends to be good programming practice, in general, to make unused fields in your packets have predictable values. It's not required by the RFC, just a good idea.

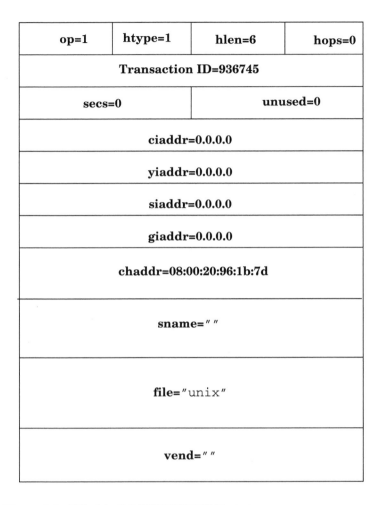

Figure 2-2 Filled-in BOOTREQUEST Packet

power is restored, all the computers try to boot at the same time, and all of them send BOOTREQUEST packets simultaneously. Naturally, there's a massive pileup on the network and only a few packets get through.

So, the 998 computers that get no BOOTREPLYs have to try again, and, say ten seconds later, they all transmit their packets *again*. We get another massive pileup, and continue with only a few computers getting their requests answered each time. And after the machines that do get their replies start trying to boot over the network, the problem just gets worse.

The BOOTP RFC recommends using a randomized backoff strategy, similar to that used in Ethernet retransmission. Each time a BOOTREPLY fails to arrive, the client should wait a longer interval before retransmitting. The time should be doubled and randomized so that all computers don't try to hit the server in lockstep.

Once the wait time reaches about one minute, it should stabilize, but still be randomized.

Nothing is going to make a thousand computers all booting over the network pleasant, but this can at least ease the pain to a tolerable level.

2.3.3 What the Server Does with the BOOTREQUEST Packet

All right, the client's carefully prepared packet eventually arrives at the server. Now what?

First, the server (or the TCP/IP protocol stack of the server host machine) performs the usual UDP packet processing. If the packet that arrived is not addressed to this machine, or to the broadcast address, it is discarded. If the UDP checksum doesn't check, the packet is discarded. If the destination port is not the BOOTP server port, the packet is discarded.[3] If there is no program, process or other entity "listening" on the BOOTP server port, the packet is discarded. In other words, if this packet was not sent to an active BOOTP server on this machine, toss the packet into the proverbial bit bucket.

If the packet passes this initial screening, it is passed along to the BOOTP server itself, which starts its own processing. First it checks the server name field (sname). If the field is empty, the client doesn't care which BOOTP server it contacts, and this server can continue processing the packet. On the other hand, if a value is specified in the field and it matches the server's name (or nickname), the client wants to contact THIS server, and the server will continue. And, if the field is set but specifies a different server, there is a question of what to do. The RFC gives three options:

1. Discard the packet. It wasn't for this server, so ignore it. This is the simplest thing to do.

2. If the name specified is known (through some lookup) to be, in some sense, local, the server can assume that the other server got it, and discard the packet. Yes, this is the same action as #1, but for a different reason. This option will probably only be implemented if #3 is also.

3. If the server is not local, that is, it is located on a network segment that would not see broadcasts on the local segment, the server can forward the packet to the correct server using unicast IP. In this case, the server should fill in the gateway IP address field (giaddr) which the remote server can use to send the reply back. The value put in giaddr can be the IP address of the local BOOTP server, or that of a gateway or router that will forward the reply back to this local network segment.

---

[3] In practice, if the destination port is not the BOOTP server port, the packet is most likely not a BOOTP packet at all, but one destined for some *other* UDP protocol like NFS or multicast audio, and will be delivered to the appropriate program. From the BOOTP server's point of view, the packet never happened. These are not the bits you're looking for. You can go about your business.

At this point, the server has decided to accept and process the BOOTRE-QUEST packet. It is convenient to imagine that at this point the server creates a BOOTREPLY packet and starts filling it in. As always, when doing any Internet programming, it's good practice to set the packet to zeros before doing anything else.

Of course, an actual implementation may not create the reply packet at this point; it could just collect the data to go into the packet and create it later. This would have the advantage that if, due to some problem discovered while processing the client's request, the server decides to discard the client packet, the cleanup is easier, since there is no half-completed reply packet to destroy.

However, we'll imagine we make the reply first and fill it as we go, to make the explanation flow smoother. If you're writing code, do whatever suits your implementation design. If you're not, then it doesn't really matter, does it?

The next thing the server does is examine the client IP address (`ciaddr`) field. If this is zero (i.e., set to the IP address 0.0.0.0), the client does not know its own IP address and wishes the server to tell it which address to use. The server should use the client's hardware address (sent in the `chaddr` field) to look in its database for the IP address that the client should use. If there is a match, the server has an IP address for the client it can place into the "Your IP Address" (`yiaddr`) field. If there is no match found, the request packet is discarded. BOOTP will not do dynamic generation of addresses; that's what DHCP is for. We'll get there in the next chapter.

Next, the filename field (`file`) is checked. If the field is not set, the client doesn't care about filenames and the server can skip to the next task. If it is set, the client wants some information. The server will use the filename field contents to match with its stored configurations. If there is a match, the stored data will tell what string should be sent back to the client. Usually this will be the full pathname of the file the client should load and run. If the string set by the client is not found in the server's store, the packet can be discarded, as it wants something the server does not have.

Now, the vendor-specific field (`vend`) can be checked and if the server recognizes the "Magic Number", it can do its vendor-specific thing and place the result in the `vend` field of the BOOTREPLY packet. Figure 2-3 shows a typical BOOTREPLY packet filled in and ready to go.

2.3.4 Sending the BOOTREPLY Packet

The server has a nice fresh BOOTREPLY packet to send to the client. Unfortunately, this packet is an IP datagram, and the client most likely doesn't yet know its IP address, and hasn't yet fully initialized its networking code. Therefore, it cannot yet receive arbitrary packets.

If the client knows its IP address, there is still a problem; the client is still not yet fully initialized. When the server issues an ARP request for the client, it needs to be able to send a reply; thus, it is a requirement for BOOTP clients that they respond to ARP queries, even before they are fully initialized.

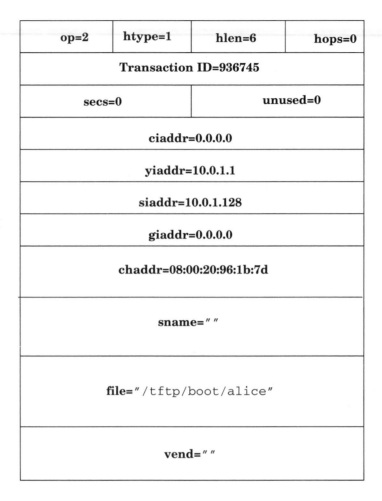

Figure 2-3 Filled-in BOOTREPLY Packet

This is, luckily, fairly easy to fold into the TCP/IP implementation needed to run the protocol anyway.

If the client does not know its IP address at this point, the server pretty much has only two choices. If it can, it can construct its own ARP table entry for the client, since the server knows the client's hardware address (Ethernet), which it remembers from the BOOTREQUEST, and it knows the client's IP address, since it just decided what it should be. Thus, the server can build its own temporary ARP entry to send the BOOTREPLY packet to the client.

Some TCP/IP implementations do not allow this kind of direct access to the ARP table, and in these cases, the server has no other choice but to broadcast the reply.

2.3.5 What the Client Does with the BOOTREPLY Packet

At last, a packet has arrived at the client. The client must now process it.

The packet is ignored if it is not addressed to the BOOTP port, or if it does not match the client's IP address (assuming the client knows its IP address)—in other words, normal UDP processing.

Next, moving into the BOOTP processing, if it is not a BOOTREPLY, or if it does not match the transaction id (xid) sent with the BOOTREQUEST, the packet is bogus and must be discarded. Otherwise, success! The client can extract its IP address from the yiaddr field and the name of its bootfile from the file field. The address of the server is in siaddr and, if giaddr is non-zero, it's the address of the first-hop router.

2.4 Routers and BOOTP

Some network managers may not wish to place a BOOTP server on every subnet in their installation. If it is desired that BOOTP work across routers, then there needs to be some cooperation from the routers.

If a router is cooperating, it will listen for BOOTREQUESTS and forward them as appropriate. It should not blindly broadcast them, but select a new network based on configuration information.

If the gateway field in the BOOTREQUEST is zero, the router must insert the IP address of the interface on which it received the packet. This will allow the server to send the reply back to the router.

The entity forwarding the BOOTP packets need not really be a router. It could be a computer that listens for BOOTREQUESTs, sends them off itself to the server (perhaps through a router), and redistributes the replies. A cute trick it can pull is to insert the local net broadcast address into the giaddr field; then the reply will come back to the "real" router and get broadcast on the local network. The drawback is that this causes more work for all hosts on the segment. These "relay agents" are discussed in detail in Chapter 6.

2.5 Summary

In this chapter, we examined the BOOTP protocol as background for the discussion of DHCP.

BOOTP is a simple request response protocol. We covered the following in regard to BOOTP:

- Transmission strategies.
- Simple error recovery.
- Packet formats.
- Data interpretation.

The DHCP Protocol

DHCP Design Goals
The DHCP "Lease"
DHCP Packet Formats
DHCP Messages
DHCP Client State Machine

DHCP was developed out of a recognition that BOOTP was inadequate to provide configuration information to computers. As computers, their operating systems, and data networks became more and more complex, the need for more configuration information grew.

DHCP, the Dynamic Host Configuration Protocol, was the result. The protocol was originally developed in 1993, defined in RFC1531 and RFC1541, and was revised in 1997. The current defining document is RFC2131.

DHCP provides two main services to network clients. First, it allocates IP network addresses to clients. These can be temporary addresses picked from a pool of available addresses by the server, or permanent ones assigned by the local system administrator and just *remembered* by the server. Second, DHCP enables the storage of parameters for clients on the network. Administrators can provide parameters for individual clients, or groups of them, and the DHCP server will store them and hand them out to clients that need to know, for example, the IP address of their default router and where to go to get X Window System fonts.

3.1 DHCP Design Goals

The designers of DHCP didn't just sit down and start coding; they had some idea of what they wanted in this protocol. Here are some of the goals set out in the RFCs:

- *Mechanism vs. policy*. The protocol should not implement any particular policy, but rather provide a flexible mechanism on which to build policy implementations.

- *No manual configuration on clients*. As far as possible, clients should just plug in and work. No intervention by an administrator to get the client up and running should be necessary.

- *One server can handle many subnets*. Many network managers don't want to dedicate a machine per subnet to providing DHCP service, so DHCP needs to work through routers, across multiple subnets.

- *Multiple servers allowed*. For redundancy and reliability, servers and clients both must be able to deal with the existence of multiple active servers on a network.

- *Statically configured hosts must coexist*. Hosts that for some reason need static IP addresses, or that cannot participate in the DHCP protocol, must be able to "live" on the same network in peace and harmony.

- *BOOTP coexistence*. DHCP implementations must interoperate with BOOTP relay agents and provide service to BOOTP clients.

- *Unique address guarantee*. DHCP must never assign the same IP address to multiple clients.

- *Retain client information*. DHCP must retain per client parameters in stable storage so that server outages will not affect the integrity of this information.

3.2   The DHCP "Lease"

Since the basic idea of DHCP is to assign IP addresses to clients, once assigned, the server needs to "remember" the assignment, along with any other parameters provided. If the client reboots and again needs an IP address, it would be nice to be able to give it the same one, if possible. This would lessen the need to flush stored data in, for example, DNS servers. Also, the server needs to keep track of what addresses have been issued so that it can avoid giving out duplicate addresses.

The association of an IP address and a client is called a *binding* in the DHCP RFC, and is also often called a *lease*; the idea is that a client "leases" an address for a given amount of time. Once that time is up, the client must relinquish the address.

The client has two timers, called the renewing timer (T1) and the rebinding timer (T2), that it uses to decide when to extend its lease. T1 must be set to go off before T2; it is common for implementations to make T1 half of T2.

At the expiration of T1, the client must attempt to extend its lease (also called "renewing the lease"); and when T1 expires, it must get a new lease (i.e., start over or "rebind" an address).

3.3 DHCP Packet Format

DHCP is, at the packet or message level, an extension of BOOTP. In fact, BOOTP clients can usually interact with DHCP servers—recall that this was one of the design goals for DHCP.

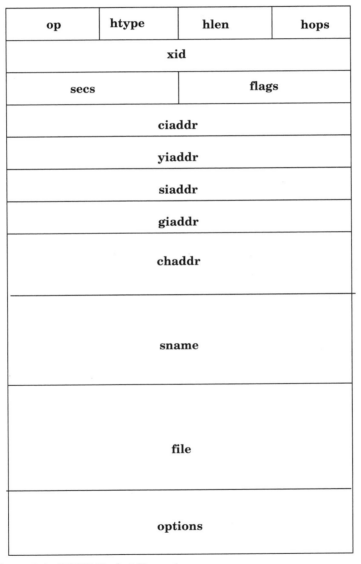

Figure 3-1 DHCP Packet Format

3.3.1 Differences from BOOTP

As shown in Figure 3-1, the fields of the DHCP packet are very similar to those in a BOOTP packet. The differences are:

op
: The op field that defines the type of a message still only has two values: 1 and 2, BOOTREQUEST and BOOTREPLY. BOOTREQUEST is used for all messages that are sent from a client to a server, and BOOTREPLY for all messages sent from a server to a client. The type of the DHCP message is carried in the options field, in an option with tag value 53. By using an option for the DHCP message type, instead of extending the op field with new values, existing BOOTP relay agents will continue to forward DHCP messages, since they all look like valid BOOTP messages, until we examine the options carefully.

flags
: The unused byte in the second word of the BOOTP packet is now called the flags field. The leftmost bit of this 16-bit field is designated the BROADCAST flag, and the remaining bits must be set to zero.
  Some client TCP/IP implementations discard all unicast IP packets until completely initialized; DHCP packets destined for these clients (which carry the very information they need to initialize!) must be broadcast. Therefore, the client in such a state should set the BROADCAST bit so that the server knows to broadcast the replies.

options
: Options are used to carry additional information specific to DHCP so as not to alter the BOOTP packet format too much. The options field is longer than the BOOTP options field, though, and is variable-sized.
  Options are a way of carrying information not foreseen by the protocol designers. Vendors that wish to provide information to their clients not designed into the protocol can use options.

Client identifier
: A new option available with DHCP is the "client identifier" option. This allows clients to be identified with a unique, opaque identifier, instead of relying on the hardware address as done in BOOTP. The client identifier can be the hardware address, but it is not required to be. A client that supports some other kind of unique identifier could use that. Sun workstations and servers have a 'hostid' for instance.
  In practice, client IDs are not used much. Hardware addresses turn out to be quite sufficient. Despite the disadvantage of getting a new address when a network card is changed, this is rare enough not to be a major problem.

3.3.2 How Options Work

The options field is encoded following the description in RFC1497, which in turn follows RFC951—our old friend, the original BOOTP document. The current list of defined options is in RFC2131.

The first four bytes of the option field should be set to a special value that tells us that this field is coded according to DHCP rules. These first four bytes should be, in decimal "99.130.83.99", or in hex "63.82.53.63".[1] This is called the "Magic Number". A "Magic Number" is one that serves to identify something, yet has no inherent meaning. Why does "99.139.83.99" identify DHCP-coded options? Magic, that's all, just magic.

Following the Magic Number come the options proper. These are implemented as a sequence of tagged data fields, wherein the first byte is called the tag and identifies the type and format of data. There are three types of tagged fields:

- Fixed-length fields with no data.
- Fixed-length fields with fixed data.
- Variable-length fields.

3.3.2.1 Fixed-length Fields with No Data

In fixed-length fields with no data, there is only a tag byte. The two tags defined for this format are:

Pad field. The pad field has tag value 0, and is used to make the following options align on word (or other desired) boundaries, which might be convenient for some types of computers. Sun SPARC processors, for example, cannot read a longword (four bytes) unless it is aligned properly in memory; therefore, if one needs to be able to read longwords with arbitrary alignments, the code must be prepared to read the bytes individually and reassemble the number "by hand". This is an example of how a little thought in designing packet layouts can lead to an enormous savings of effort in coding the software.

The pad field can be considered to be a "no-op" for DHCP options, rather like the "no-op" instruction most computers have built in. It seems useless, but is actually quite useful.

End field. The end field has tag value 255, and is used to indicate the end of useful data in the options field. The rest of the options field should be filled with zeros, following the "if it's not used, fill it with zeros" principal. (The zeros happen to be ignorable "pad" options, which is not a coincidence.)

This field must be present if there are any options at all, and it must come last, since everything after it will be ignored.

---

[1] Of course, the same values will be stored in the packet whether we display them in decimal, hex, binary, or roman numerals. 99 decimal, 63 hex, and LXXXXIX all produce the same bit pattern on the wire or in the RAM.

3.3.2.2 Fixed-length Fields with Fixed Data

Fixed-length fields that actually have data are coded with one byte of tag, one byte of length, and then the appropriate number of bytes of data.

Subnet mask field. The subnet mask field holds the local subnet mask. The tag value is 1 and the length is 4. Thus, the entire subnet mask field occupies 6 bytes.

Time offset field. The tag value is 2 and the length is 4 bytes. This field is a signed 32-bit integer in network byte order holding the time offset of the local net in seconds from Coordinated Universal Time (UTC).

3.3.2.3 Variable-length Fields

The remaining fields are variable-length data fields, with one byte of tag, one byte of length, and length bytes of data. This means that there can be at most 256 tags, and the maximum length of a data field can be 256 bytes.

All the options currently defined are shown in Appendix B. Option tag values 128-254 are reserved. Option tag values 53-61 are used by the DHCP protocol.

3.4 DHCP Messages

A flow of packets containing *DHCP messages* implements the DHCP protocol. A DHCP message is a BOOTP packet that contains a DHCP Message Type option. A typical exchange of messages is shown in Figure 3-3.

Here are the types of messages defined for DHCP:

3.4.1 DHCPDISCOVER

The first type of message is DHCPDISCOVER, which a client broadcasts to find its local DHCP servers. The Message Type option is coded '1'.

3.4.2 DHCPOFFER

DHCP servers that receive a client's DHCPDISCOVER, and which can service the request for information, send a DHCPOFFER to the client with a set of parameters. The Message Type option is coded '2'.

3.4.3 DHCPREQUEST

The client receives one or more DHCPOFFERs, and decides which offer to accept. It then sends a DHCPREQUEST offer to the lucky "winner". All other servers see this broadcast message and can deduce that they are "losers". The Message Type option is coded '3'.

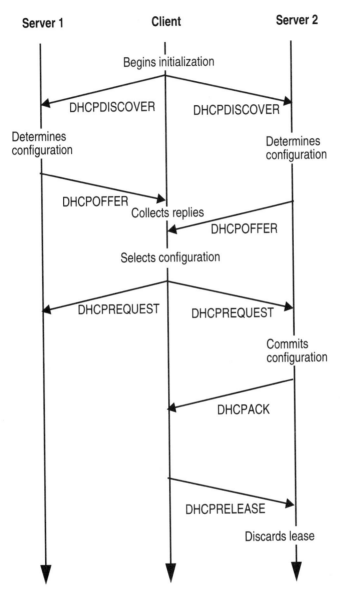

Figure 3-2 DHCP Typical Message Flow

3.4.4 **DHCPACK**

Finally, the server sends a DHCPACK to the client with the full set of configuration parameters, confirming to the client that it got the DHCPREQUEST, and providing the complete set of needed information. The "ACK" part of this message name comes from "acknowledge". The Message Type option is coded '5'.

3.4.5 DHCPNAK

If the client has requested (with a DHCPREQUEST message) an address that is incorrect, expired, or otherwise unacceptable, the server sends a DHCP-NAK to the client to tell it, "No, sorry, you can't have that address."

"NAK", in this case, comes from "negative acknowledge". The Message Type option is coded '5'.

3.4.6 DHCPDECLINE

If the client gets an offered address, and subsequently discovers that the address is already in use elsewhere in the network, it should send a DHCPDE-CLINE to the server. The client might try sending a ping to the address; if it gets a reply, someone out there is using the address the server thought was available. The Message Type option is coded '4'.

3.4.7 DHCPRELEASE

When a client no longer needs to use a dynamically assigned address, it should send a DHCPRELEASE message to the server to let the server know the address is no longer being used. Not all DHCP clients do this since it is technically optional. The Message Type option is coded '7'.

3.4.8 DHCPINFORM

If a client already has an IP address, but still needs some configuration information, the DHCPINFORM message will serve the task. The Message Type option is coded '8'.

3.5 DHCP Client State Machine

Now we see why state machines were described in Chapter 1. In Figure 3-3, we see the state diagram that represents the client side of the DHCP protocol, and how and when the messages flow. You can compare this diagram to the message flow diagram (Figure 3-2) and see how the client changes state as the messages move.

3.5.1 INIT

All clients start in the INIT (for "initial") state. The only action performed in the INIT state is the sending of a DHCPDISCOVER message, whereupon the client moves to the SELECTING state.

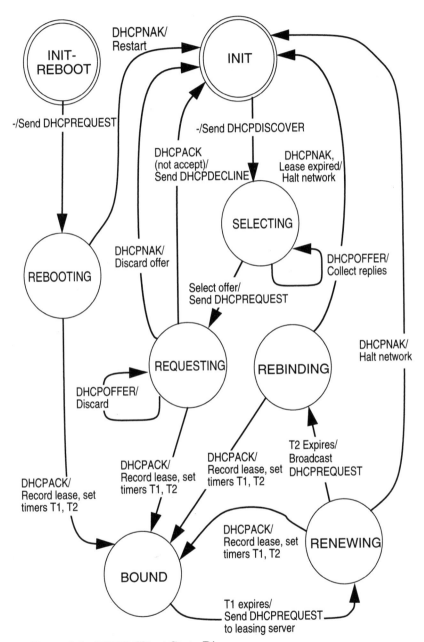

Figure 3-3 DHCP Client State Diagram

3.5.2 SELECTING

In the SELECTING state, the client collects DHCPOFFER messages from servers that care to reply to the DHCPDISCOVER. The idea that messages are collected implies a waiting period after which the client will assume that no more DHCPOFFERS are going to arrive. This waiting period is not specified by the RFCs, and protocol implementors are free to choose a "reasonable" period.

Since the state diagram shows a transition arrow for each type of message that could be received and acted on by the client, there is a transition shown for these DHCPOFFER messages, which takes the client right back into the same state. This type of transition is common in these diagrams, and serves to indicate both that the message associated with the transition *is* relevant to this state, and that the protocol designer has in fact *not* forgotten about this case.

Once the client decides that it has waited long enough and collected enough DHCPOFFER messages, it selects one and sends a DHCPREQUEST message to the appropriate server, moving into the REQUESTING state.

It is acceptable for the waiting period to be zero, and for the client to act on the first message it receives. How the client decides which of the multiple offers to accept will be discussed in Chapter 4.

3.5.3 REQUESTING

Once a client has decided on which offer to accept, has sent a DHCPRE-QUEST to the winning server, and is in the REQUESTING state, all further DHCPOFFER messages that might arrive are discarded. Other than that, three things can now happen.

First, if the server has changed its mind (or rather, has changed circumstances since it sent the DHCPOFFER, for whatever reason) and cannot fulfill its offer, then it will send the client a DHCPNAK message, basically saying, "The deal's off". The client must now discard the offer, return to the INIT state, and start over.

Second, the server could send a DHCPACK message that is unacceptable to the client, usually because the address turns out to already be in use elsewhere. The client must then send a DHCPDECLINE message ("Thanks anyway, but no thanks") and also return to the INIT state and start over.

Third, if the server sends an acceptable DHCPACK, the client can make note of the fact that it now has a lease on this address for a given time (specified in the DHCPACK). It can use the configuration parameters supplied, and it can start the T1 and T2 timers. It now moves to the BOUND state.

3.5.4 BOUND

The BOUND state is where a client will spend most of its time, happily using the configuration supplied by the server and doing (it is hoped) useful work for its owner.

The client leaves the BOUND state when the timer T1 expires. It then sends a new DHCPREQUEST to the server it got its address from, and moves to the RENEWING state.

3.5.5 RENEWING

In the RENEWING state, the client is attempting to negotiate an extension of its lease. It has sent a DHCPREQUEST to the server it got its address from, and is waiting for a reply. Three things can now happen.

First, if the server denies the extension and sends a DHCPNAK message, the client is in trouble, network-wise. It must abandon use of the address, halt all network traffic, and enter the INIT state, starting over again from the beginning.

Second, if the timer T2 expires and the server has not replied to the DHCPREQUEST, the client broadcasts a DHCPREQUEST and enters the REBINDING state, where it attempts to negotiate a new address lease with any server it can find.

Finally, and much preferred, if the server replies with a DHCPACK, the lease is extended and the client can reset the timers and continue, moving back to the BOUND state.

3.5.6 REBINDING

If the T2 timer expires while in the RENEWING state, the client enters the REBINDING state and sends a broadcast request for a new lease. In this state, one of two things can happen.

The client can get a DHCPACK indicating that the request is approved and the lease is extended, whereupon it moves back to BOUND and resets its timers, or it can get a DHCPNAK indicating the opposite: Request denied, give up your address, go to INIT to start over, have a nice day.

3.5.7 INIT-REBOOT

If the client starts up knowing its network address, possibly assigned during a previous DHCP session, it begins in the special INIT-REBOOT state. It immediately sends a DHCPREQUEST to the server it got its address from asking if it can please continue to use the address, and moves to the REBOOTING state.

3.5.8 REBOOTING

The REBOOTING state is very much like REBINDING, except for the implicit knowledge that the machine is reinitializing and previously had a valid lease on an address. Like REBINDING, two things are possible.

The server could decide it's okay and send a DHCPACK. The client then notes the lease information, resets the timers T1 and T2, and continues to initialize.

However, the server could decide that continued use of the address is not okay. If the client was turned off for a long time, the server might have decided the client was gone and reassigned the address. Also, the client might have been turned off and moved to a different subnet, where it will need a different address. Whatever the reason, the server sends a DHCPNAK and the client has to go to the INIT state and start over, getting a lease "the hard way" instead of keeping its old one.

3.6 Summary

This chapter presented the DHCP protocol itself. We reviewed the design goals of the protocol and examined the concept of a DHCP lease. A discussion of the packet formats and how they differ from BOOTP was next, followed by a detailed description of the DHCP message formats. Finally, a look at the client state machine wrapped up the chapter.

DHCP Operations:
The Client's View

So far, we've seen how the BOOTP proto-col works and how it was extended to form DHCP. Now we'll examine the common operations that DHCP clients perform, and see the details of how the protocol works.

4.1 Getting a Lease

The first and most common operation a DHCP client performs is getting a lease on an IP address. To do this, it must:

- Find DHCP servers.
- Tell the DHCP servers its need.
- Get offers from the servers.
- Pick an offer.
- Request that an offer be confirmed.
- Get an acknowledgment.
- Configure itself.

To perform these operations, the client follows the state machine shown in Chapter 3. Depending on what happened last, it starts in either the INIT or INIT-REBOOT state, and if it follows the rules, it should get what it wants.

The client should wait a little while—the RFC recommends between one and ten seconds—before starting the process, so that if, say, a thousand clients all power up simultaneously after a power failure, the poor server isn't swamped with a thousand simultaneous requests, nor is the LAN hammered with a packet storm from all clients trying to transmit at once.

Example. In this section we'll watch Alice (host A in our sample network) try to get an IP address from a server. We'll assume that Xavier and Zelda (servers X and Z) are both running DHCP servers, and that router R has an active relay agent.

4.1.1 Tell the DHCP Server What It Needs

The first thing for the client to do is to assemble information to tell the servers enough that they can fulfill the client's request. The client forms a packet with the data, and sends it as shown below.

The client starts in the INIT state, and builds a DHCPDISCOVER packet. The protocol standard requires that the packet contain:

- BOOTREQUEST in the `op` field.
- 0.0.0.0 in the client address (`ciaddr`) field.
- The client's MAC address, MAC address length, and type in the `chaddr`, `hlen`, and `htype` fields, respectively.
- A DHCP Message Type option coded as "DHCPDISCOVER" (Option 53).
- A "randomly" selected transaction identifier in the `xid` field.

Optionally, the client can include:

- A unique ID, not necessarily the MAC address, in the Client Identifier option (Option 61).
- A request for specific parameters with the Parameter Request List option (Option 55). If such a list is placed in the DHCPDISCOVER message, it must be included in all further messages in the transaction.
- An option representing the client's "vendor class" (Vendor Class Identifier option, Option 60).
- A request for a specific IP address with a Requested IP Address option (Option 50).
- A request for a specific lease time with an IP Address Lease Time option (Option 51).
- Maximum Message Size option.
- Site-specific option.
- Other optional options.

All other fields not mentioned, or optional fields not used, should be filled with zeros. If the options overflow the `options` field, the Options Overload option (Option 52) must be used (*in* the `options` field) to indicate which of the `file` and `sname` fields also hold options.

Upon sending the DHCPDISCOVER, host A moves to the SELECTING state.

Example. Host A (Alice) might fill out a DHCPDISCOVER packet like this:

op:tu:ln:hops	xid	secs flag	ciaddr
01:01:06:00	12345678	0000:8000	0.0.0.0

yiaddr · siaddr · giaddr · chaddr

yiaddr	siaddr	giaddr	chaddr
0.0.0.0	0.0.0.0	0.0.0.0	01:23:45:00

chaddr (continued) · sname

chaddr (continued)			sname
01:01:00:00	00:00:00:00	00:00:00:00	00...

sname... · file...

sname...		file...	
00...		00...	

options...

options...			
63.82.53.63	35:01:01 FF	00...	

(Each box is 32 bits, and each line is 16 bytes of packet. Numbers are in hexadecimal, except IP addresses. The `sname`, `file`, and `options` fields are truncated to save space, and filled with zeros where not otherwise specified.) This packet has the Broadcast flag on (high bit of `flags` field), zeros for all IP addresses, and contains two options after the DHCP Magic Cookie (`63.82.53.63`): the DHCP Message Type option (Option 53, 35 in hex), which indicates this is a DHCPDISCOVER (message type 01), and the obligatory END option, showing the end of the options.

Client Alice then sends this packet to the DHCP servers, as detailed below.

4.1.2 Finding DHCP Servers

Finding DHCP servers is actually quite easy. The client merely broadcasts the initial DHCPDISCOVER packet on its local network segment. This is an IP broadcast; that is, the destination address in the IP packet is `255.255.255.255`. The data part of the packet is contained in the UDP packet, which is sent to UDP Port 67, the "well-known" DHCP server port.

This broadcast will be received by all DHCP servers and relay agents on the local segment; the relay agents will forward the packet to its remote DHCP server as appropriate.

Now technically, the client hasn't yet "found" any servers at all, since it has no knowledge of the identity of any DHCP servers; but, it has managed to get its message to them, which is what counts at this point.

Example. Host A forms a DHCPDISCOVER packet (as detailed in the next section) and broadcasts it on subnet 10.0.1.0. Server X receives it and starts doing its DHCP thing with it. Router R receives it and forwards it to server Z on subnet 10.0.2.0. (Hosts B and C also receive the broadcast packet, but since they have no programs listening on UDP Port 67, they discard it.)

4.1.3 Get Offers from the Servers

While in the SELECTING state, the client collects offers from the various servers in the form of DHCPOFFER packets. It waits "a while" to make sure that it gets "all" of the offers. How long it waits is not specified in any standards documents, but is left up to the implementor to decide. It is entirely acceptable to merely wait until the first DHCPOFFER arrives, or to wait one second, or one minute. The longer the waiting time, of course, the more annoyed the human being waiting for the machine to initialize is going to be; but the shorter the time, the more likely it is that the client will miss some DHCPOFFERs.

While waiting, the client must throw away any packets whose transaction id (xid) does not match the one they sent in the original DHCPDISCOVER packet. Any type of DHCP message other than a DHCPOFFER will also be thrown away.

Example. In our example, server X picks an IP address that is free for its subnet, perhaps 10.0.1.32. How it decides on this will be explained in the next chapter. It forms a DHCPOFFER packet and sends it to host A.

Server Z also picks an IP address for host A, perhaps 10.0.2.45, and sends it to A through the relay agent on router R. Host A collects these offers for an "implementation-dependent" time, all while remaining in the SELECTING state.

4.1.4 Pick an Offer

Having received at least one, and possibly many DHCPOFFER packets, the client must pick one to respond to. Again, the criteria used to select one of the offers is not specified by any standard, and is left up to the implementor. A common scheme is to simply pick the one that arrives first.

A client could use the offered lease times, knowledge of network topology, or the phase of the moon and its user's favorite color to make the decision.

Example. In our example, client A has received the following offers:

Client A gets this packet from server X:

op:tu:ln:hops	xid	secs flag	ciaddr
01:01:06:00	12:34:56:78	0000:8000	0.0.0.0
yiaddr	siaddr	giaddr	chaddr
10.0.2.32	0.0.0.0	0.0.0.0	01:23:45:00
chaddr (continued)			sname
01:01:00:00	00:00:00:00	00:00:00:00	00...
sname...		file....	
00...		00...	
options...			
63.82.53.63	35:01:05 33	04:00:01:51	80 36:04:10
more options...			
0.1.128 FF	00 00...		

The offered IP address is 10.0.1.32 in the `yiaddr` field; the offered lease time is one day (86,400 (15180hex) seconds in the second option: Option 51 = 33hex); and the server's IP address of 10.0.1.128[1] is in the third option (Option 54 = 36hex).

The packet client A gets from server Z looks like this:

op:tu:ln:hops	xid	secs flag	ciaddr
01:01:06:00	12:34:56:78	0000:8000	0.0.0.0
yiaddr	siaddr	giaddr	chaddr
10.0.2.45	0.0.0.0	0.0.0.0	01:23:45:00
chaddr (continued)			sname
01:01:00:00	00:00:00:00	00:00:00:00	00...
sname...		file....	
00...		00...	
options...			
63.82.53.63	35:01:02 33	04:00:00:02	58 36:04:10
more options...			
0.2.128 FF	00 00...		

We can see the offered address of 10.0.2.45 in the `yiaddr` field, the offered lease time of ten minutes (600 seconds) in the second option, and the server's IP address of 10.0.2.128 in the third option.

Continuing the example, let's have client A choose server X's offer because it has a longer lease time (86400 seconds, or one day) than server Z's offer.

4.1.5 Request the Offered Address

Having picked one of the offers, the client now builds and sends a DHCPREQUEST packet to claim the offered address. After the DHCPRE-QUEST is sent, the client moves to the REQUESTING state, and any further DHCPOFFERs that arrive are discarded.

DHCPREQUEST packets are usually broadcast, so that all servers involved are aware of which offer the client has chosen.

Example. Client A builds the following packet to respond to client X's offers:

---

[1] A high-quality implementation would probably add pad options so as to have the server IP address and 4-byte offered lease time fall on 4-byte boundaries.

op:tu:ln:hops	xid	secs flag	ciaddr
01:01:06:00	12:34:56:78	0000:8000	0.0.0.0
yiaddr	**siaddr**	**giaddr**	**chaddr**
10.0.2.45	0.0.0.0	0.0.0.0	01:23:45:00
chaddr (continued)			**sname**
01:01:00:00	00:00:00:00	00:00:00:00	00...
sname...		**file....**	
00...		00...	
options...			
63.82.53.63	35:01:02 33	04:00:01:51	80 36:04:10
more options...			
0.1.128 FF	00 00...		

In this packet, the options included are:

- DHCP Message Type, DHCPREQUEST (35:01:02).
- IP Address Lease Time, 86400 seconds (33:04:00:01:51:80).
- Server ID, 10.0.1.128 (36:04:10.0.1.128).
- End of options (FF).

The rest of the options field should be filled with zeros.

If the client had sent a Parameter Request List option (Option 55) in the original DHCPDISCOVER message, it must repeat the same option in this message.

4.1.6 Await Acknowledgment

Now the client waits for the DHCP server to do its server thing and send back an acknowledgment. When the acknowledgment, in the form of a DHCP-ACK message, arrives, the client can believe that it has a valid lease on the IP address and can use the information.

Example. Server X sends back this packet as a DHCPACK.

op:tu:ln:hops	xid	secs flag	ciaddr
01:01:06:00	12:34:56:78	0000:8000	0.0.0.0
yiaddr	**siaddr**	**giaddr**	**chaddr**
10.0.2.45	0.0.0.0	0.0.0.0	01:23:45:00
chaddr (continued)			**sname**
01:01:00:00	00:00:00:00	00:00:00:00	00...
sname...		**file....**	
00...		00...	
options...			
63.82.53.63	35:01:05 33	04:00:01:51	80 36:04:10
more options...			
1.2.128 FF	00 00...		

The options included here are:

- DHCP message, DHCPACK (`35:04:05`).
- IP lease time, 86400 seconds (`33:04:00:01:51:80`).
- Server ID (...).
- End option (`FF`).

4.1.7 Configure

The client now has the information it needs to configure itself. It sets its IP address according to the information in the DHCPACK packet, and starts timers T1 and T2 so that it can renew when necessary. The T1 timer is usually set to about half the lease time, and the T2 timer to about 7/8 of the lease time. Use of T1 and T2 is described in the next section.

It stores the address of the server from which it got the lease, and finally enters the BOUND state, where it stays for most of the time it's running.

Example. Finally, the client can extract the information from the packet and configure itself. It sets its IP address to 10.0.2.45, the T1 timer to 43,200 seconds (half of the offered lease time of 24 hours), and the T2 timer to 86,400 seconds (one day).

If any optional parameters are delivered, now is the time to decode and use them.

4.2 Renewing and Rebinding

When the timer T1 goes off (however that is arranged in the operating system in use), it's time to start trying to convince the server to extend the lease.

T1 must be set to expire some time before T2, and T2 in turn must be set to expire before the lease expires. It is common (but not required) for T1 to be 1/2 of the lease time, and T2 to be about 7/8 of it. The RFC recommends that these times be chosen with a bit of variance, so that clients that boot at the same time won't all renew at the same time. The server can force a client to set these timers to particular values by using the Renewal (T1) Time Value option (Option 58) and the Rebinding (T2) Time Value option (Option 59).

When T1 expires, the client moves to the RENEWING state, and sends a DHCPREQUEST to the server it obtained the lease from. The client must put its current IP address in the client address field (`ciaddr`) of the DHCPREQUEST packet. If it gets a DHCPACK back from the server, it updates T1 and T2 with new values derived from the new IP lease time, and moves back to the BOUND state.

If no response comes in a reasonable time (where "reasonable" is defined by the implementation; a few seconds to a minute or two seems reasonable to me), the client should wait about half the time left until T2 is scheduled to expire and resend the DHCPREQUEST. If there is still no response from the server, the client should halve the time to wait and resend again, continuing until it gets down to about a minute and then just let T2 expire.

If the server does not respond with an ACK before T2 goes off, the client moves into the REBINDING state and *broadcasts* a DHCPREQUEST so that any server can give it a new lease. If it gets a DHCPACK from a server, it can reset its timers T1 and T2 and continue; if, however, it gets a DHCPNAK, it must consider its lease expired and "move out" by shutting down network services, moving to the INIT state, and starting all over again.

If no reply is received at all by the time the lease expires, the client must also shut down its network, move to the INIT state, and start over.

4.3   Reusing a Lease

If a client initializes and discovers that it was previously issued a lease on an address, and it wishes to reuse that old address, it is possible for it to request a lease on the particular address. Many servers will permit this, as it's generally desirable to avoid gratuitously changing a client's IP address.

If a client is attempting to reuse a previously assigned address, it skips the "discover" phase of the DHCP process, and immediately sends a DHCPRE-QUEST. The Requested IP Address option will have the address it is trying to verify, and the `ciaddr` field must be zero.

If the server denies the request, the client must go to the INIT state and request an address "from scratch". The server could deny the request because the address has already been handed out, the client has moved to a different subnet on which the address is invalid, or for any other reason.

If the address is still available, and the client is still in the right place, the server can reply with a DHCPACK, and the client can go ahead and configure itself, as above.

4.4   Releasing a Lease

If a client knows that it is shutting down in an orderly manner and does not want to reuse an address, it can inform the server by sending a DHCPRELEASE message. This message must be unicast to the server the lease was obtained from.

Example. If Alice was shutting down and wanted to abandon the lease on the address obtained from server Xavier, the following DHCPRELEASE packet would be sent:

op:tu:ln:hops	xid	secs flag	ciaddr
01:01:06:00	12:34:56:78	0000:8000	0.0.0.0

yiaddr	siaddr	giaddr	chaddr
10.0.2.45	0.0.0.0	0.0.0.0	01:23:45:00

chaddr (continued)			sname
01:01:00:00	00:00:00:00	00:00:00:00	00...

sname...		file....	
00...		00...	

options...			
63.82.53.63	35:01:07 36	04:10 1.2.128	FF 00...

more options...			
00...			

4.5 Getting Other Parameters

Many parameters are needed for configuring modern, Internet-capable clients. The addresses of the default routers and nameservers are essential for TCP/IP; there are similar parameters for other applications like the X Window System, Network Time Protocol or email, or other protocols like NetBIOS, Novell IPX, and so on.

These can be fetched using the Parameter Request List option (Option 55). If a given parameter has an option, defined either by the IETF in one of the RFC documents, or by the equipment vendor as a proprietary extension, the client can ask that the server supply the appropriate parameters in the replies by sending a Parameter Request List option in the first DHCPDISCOVER message. Servers will send back such values as they can supply in the DHCPOFFER, and if the client needs to choose between multiple offers, it can use the presence or absence of its necessary parameters as one of the criteria it uses to choose between them.

The Parameter Request List option has a variable length, and the data are just a list of the option codes for the desired parameters.

Example. If a client needed the addresses of a default router (Option 3) and a SMTP server (Option 69), it would code a Parameter Request List option as 37:02:03:45 (55:2:3:69 in decimal). The bytes are, in order, the option code for the Parameter Request List option, the length (two, for two bytes of option codes), and then the two option codes, 3 and 69.

The client must send the same Parameter Request List option in the DHCPREQUEST message that it used in the DHCPDISCOVER, and it must specify the desired parameters in the same order. Servers do not need to supply all of the requested parameters, but the ones they do supply must be in the same order as the requests in the Parameter Request List option. This is mainly to make implementation somewhat easier.

Most servers allow the network manager to specify parameters for groups of clients; for example, one might be able to specify that clients on *this* subnet get *that* DNS server, or that clients with *this* MAC address get *those* IP addresses.

Finally, what if a client already has an IP address, can talk on the local network just fine, but just needs to fetch some of these parameters so it can finish configuring itself? It can't use DHCPDISCOVER, since it doesn't want an IP address, and it can't use DHCPREQUEST, as from the INIT-REBOOT state: Since the server didn't issue the address, it will of course send back a DHCPNAK.

The DHCPINFORM message was invented to solve just this situation. The client fills in the client address field (`ciaddr`), adds a Parameter Request List option, and broadcasts it on the local network. If a server receives it, it replies with a DHCPACK to the `ciaddr` address, and supplies any of the desired options it can. It must not check that the IP address has a valid lease, or fill in the "your IP address" field (`yiaddr`); "Just the options" is all it can send back.

4.6 Errors, or What To Do When You Don't Get What You Want

Part of good protocol design is dealing with errors, or unexpected events. If no events are unexpected, or at least no events are unplanned for, we can have a robust protocol. Most possible "errors", such as getting a DHCPNAK when you expect something else, are discussed in the appropriate section.

4.6.1 No Offers Ever Come

One possible error condition occurs when a client sends a DHCPDIS-COVER and nothing comes back. From the client's point of view, it's unclear *why* nothing is coming back. The server could be down; or, the server could be up but the router between could be down. Whatever the reason, all the poor client really knows is that it sent its properly formatted DHCPDISCOVER message out, and after some time period of waiting to collect DHCPOFFERs, none have come back.

In this circumstance, the client's choices are restricted to:

1. Wait some more. This is not likely to be fruitful if the waiting period is already "long enough" that the server should have replied long since, if it was going to.
2. Try again, i.e., send out a new DHCPDISCOVER. This is a reasonable thing to try; perhaps the crashed server will restart, and all will be okay. But, if a more persistent failure has occurred, such as a comet smashing the city the server is in[2], then it isn't going to come back.
3. Give up and report failure. Sometimes you just can't win.

---

[2] Hey, I saw it in a movie. Two movies! It *could* happen!

4.6.2 Badly Formed or Garbled Packet

If a packet makes it through the protocol stack and is delivered to the DHCP client, but makes no sense, it should be discarded, perhaps with a warning to the user. Possible causes of this include:

- Incorrect transaction ID field (xid).
- No DHCP Message Type option.
- DHCP message type inappropriate for current state.
- Required fields not filled in (see Tables 4-1 and 4-2).
- Unused fields have data (unused bits in flags field, for example).

It is a good idea when implementing, to remember the IETF maxim: "Be conservative in what you send and liberal in what you accept."

4.6.3 REQUEST Sent, But DHCPACK Unacceptable

If the server sends back a DHCPACK that has unacceptable parameters (perhaps we really need an X Window System font server address, but the DHCP server has not been configured to supply one), then what happens is up to the client implementation. Depending on the nature of the required parameters, it may not be able to finish configuring, or it may be able to initialize and operate in a degraded configuration. In either case, warning the user is a very good idea. Human intervention is probably now required.

4.7 Summary of Fields and Options

Table 4-1 presents a summary of the fields in a DHCP client message, and what should go in each depending on the type of DHCP message.

Table 4-2 presents the options that can go in client messages. Following IETF usage, the terms "MAY", "MUST", "MUST NOT", "SHOULD", and "SHOULD NOT" are used to indicate whether a given option is required in a given message type, forbidden, merely allowed, or recommended.

4.8 Summary

This chapter presented the way DHCP clients should behave. We covered how to get a lease on an IP address from a server, as well as how to renew, rebind, reuse, and release a lease.

How to get necessary configuration parameters was the next topic, followed by what to do if things don't go right. A summary of which fields and options are required or optional for each type of message a client can send ended the chapter.

Table 4-1 Fields of DHCP Client Messages

Field	DHCPDISCOVER	DHCPREQUEST	DHCPINFORM	DHCPRELEASE	DHCPDECLINE
op	BOOTREQUEST	BOOTREQUEST	BOOTREQUEST	BOOTREQUEST	BOOTREQUEST
htype	From "Assigned Numbers" RFC				
hlen	Hardware address length in octets				
hops	0	0	0	0	0
xid	Client-selected	From DHCPOFFER	Client-selected	Client-selected	Client-selected
secs	Seconds from DHCP start, or 0				
flags	BROADCAST flag, if required				
ciaddr	0	0	0	0	0
yiaddr	0	0	0	0	0
siaddr	0	0	0	0	0
giaddr	0	0	0	0	0
chaddr	Client's hardware address				
sname	Options or unused	Options or unused		Unused	Unused
file	Options or unused	Options or unused		Unused	Unused
options	Options	Options	Options	Unused	Unused

Table 4-2 DHCP Client Message Options

Option	DHCPDISCOVER	DHCPINFORM	DHCPREQUEST	DHCPDECLINE	DHCPRELEASE
Request IP Address	MAY	MUST NOT	MUST NOT (unless SELECTING or INIT-REBOOT, then MUST)	MUST	MUST NOT
IP Address Lease Time	MAY	MUST NOT	MAY	MUST NOT	MUST NOT
Use file/sname Fields	MAY	MAY	MAY	MAY	MAY
DHCP Message Type	DHCPDISCOVER	DHCPINFORM	DHCPREQUEST	DHCPDECLINE	DHCPRELEASE
Client Identifier	MAY	MAY	MAY	MAY	MAY
Vendor Class Identifier	MAY	MAY	MAY	MUST NOT	MUST NOT
Server Identifier	MUST NOT	MUST NOT	MUST NOT (unless SELECTING, then MUST)	MUST	MUST
Parameter Request List	MAY	MAY	MAY	MUST NOT	MUST NOT
Maximum Message Size	MAY	MAY	MAY	MUST NOT	MUST NOT
Message	SHOULD NOT	SHOULD NOT	SHOULD NOT	SHOULD	SHOULD
Site-specific	MAY	MAY	MAY	MUST NOT	MUST NOT
All others	MAY	MAY	MAY	MUST NOT	MUST NOT

DHCP Operations:
The Server's View

Assigning Address Leases

Expiring a Lease

Static IP Assignments

Summary of Fields and Options

Now we'll take a look at what the server does. In one sense, it's very simple: The server answers client requests. But in another sense, it's more complicated, but then everything is always more complicated the closer you look at it, so we won't worry.

There are a number of tasks a DHCP server must perform.

- **Assign addresses.** The server must receive packets from clients wishing to configure themselves, and assign them addresses and other configuration parameters.

- **Expire addresses.** The server must keep track of the addresses it assigns, and when the term of a lease is up, mark the address as "expired" and ready for reuse.

- **Perform BOOTP as well.** Since a design goal of DHCP was backward compatibility with BOOTP, the server must implement that protocol as well.

- **Maintain databases.** The server must keep track of all these data somehow, in such a way that if the server program is stopped and restarted, it will be able to recreate the current state of the world.

- **Report to network manager.** It is not required by the standard, but nearly every network manager wants some way of finding out what's going on in the network, and in the DHCP server. If the manager cannot get answers to questions like "How many addresses are leased, or free?",

"Which subnets have the heaviest usage?" or "Why was client C denied a lease?", then the server will not be considered as favorably as one that lets management information be easily obtained.

5.1 Assigning Address Leases

The most common operation a DHCP server performs is the assignment of an IP address for a time—a lease.

Remember that the sequence of messages involved in getting an address are:

- Client sends DHCPDISCOVER.
- Server sends DHCPOFFER.
- Client sends DHCPREQUEST.
- Server sends DHCPACK.

Once the server has sent the DHCPACK, it regards the address as "in use" and records the fact in the local database it keeps.

5.1.1 Preliminaries: Address Pools

DHCP servers must be configured with information about which networks or subnetworks they are to control, and what ranges of IP addresses can be used for dynamic assignment. If the server were to assign addresses that duplicate those of existing machines, chaos could result on the network—chaos that is pretty hard to track down. Therefore, a range of addresses must be reserved for the exclusive use of the DHCP server. Table 5-1 shows the addresses available on our sample network.

Example: In our sample network, we have two subnets: 10.0.1.0 and 10.0.2.0. If we allow machines A, B, C, and D to have dynamically assigned addresses, then the only addresses we cannot use are the broadcast address, those of the servers, and the addresses of each interface of the router. The addresses ending in 128 (for the servers), 254 (for the router), and 255 (for broadcast) cannot be used.

Table 5-1 Address Ranges Available for Assignment

Subnet	Low Address	High Address
10.0.1.0	10.0.1.1	10.0.1.127
	10.0.1.129	10.0.1.253
10.0.2.0	10.0.2.1	10.0.2.127
	10.0.2.129	10.0.2.253

A real-world network would most likely have more permanently assigned addresses than this artificial example.

The IP address ranges are configured in the server by the network manager; how this is done depends on the particular server in use.

5.1.2 DHCPDISCOVER

When the server first receives a DHCPDISCOVER message, it asks several questions:

Is this request from a network I administer?

The server must determine what subnet the client's request came from, so it can assign an appropriate address. Looking at our sample network, if server Z gets a request from client B, it should give B an address from the 10.0.1.0 subnet, not the 10.0.2.0 subnet that Z itself is connected to.

A DHCP server can easily tell which subnet a request came from. Remember that the client fills the gateway address field (`giaddr`) in the request with a zero. When a relay agent in a router forwards a DHCP message, it fills in the `giaddr` field with its own address, so that the messages for the client can be sent back there (more details in Chapter 6, DHCP Relay Agents). The server deduces the original subnet from the address of the relay agent.

Once it knows the subnet the request came from, the server can look in the table of subnets it controls, and decide if this request is worthy of consideration.

Do I have an address to give to this client?

The DHCP RFC recommends that addresses be chosen as follows:

- Use the current lease. If the client has an active lease on an address, and the request is coming from the same subnet, then give the client that address. In this case, the client is most likely renewing an existing lease.
- If there is no currently active lease, but the client had a lease before on this same subnet that it previously released or that expired, then if that previous address is still available, give it to the client.
- If the client asked for a certain address with a Requested IP Address option, and that address is available and appropriate to the subnet, then go ahead and let it have that address.
- Otherwise, pick a new address from the pool reserved for the subnet the request came from.

If the server cannot find an address for the client, it should merely decline to send a message back and discard the client's message. The client may get offers from other servers, which is fine, or it may get no offers at all, which will lead to an unhappy user. This, however, is an administrative problem, not a technical one, so we won't address it here. It would be helpful, though, for the server to log the event, so that if there was some configuration problem in the network, it would be easier to track down.

Once the server has picked an address, it chooses a lease expiration time. If the client already has an assigned network address, and isn't requesting a specific lease, then the server should use the previously assigned lease time. If there is no assigned network address, then the default lease time assigned by the network manager is used. However, if the client is requesting a specific lease, then the server gets to choose. If the address in the requested lease is available, the server can reassign it and use the previous lease time, otherwise it can make a new lease and use the default lease time.

Next, the server determines which additional parameters it should supply to the client. Besides the required IP address and lease time, the server must examine the list supplied by the client in a Parameter Request List option (Option 55). For each requested parameter, the server supplies either the local default value configured by the network manager, or the "standard" default value as defined in RFC1122 and RFC1123 (called the "Host Requirements" documents). If there is neither a configured value nor a "Host Requirements"-specified value, the server must ignore the client's request and return nothing for that parameter.

The values configured by the network manager are often assigned based on the subnet address. For example, the default router address for each subnet in the installation could be different, or the time offset could be different if some subnets are in different time zones.

If there is an existing lease, with parameters that differ from the "Host Requirements" defaults, they should be supplied. If there are parameters for this particular client configured by the network manager (recall that the client can be identified by either the client hardware address field (chaddr) or the Client Identifier option from the DHCPDISCOVER message), then those should be used in constructing the reply.

Similarly, if the client sent a Vendor Class identifier option in the message, and parameters are configured for that vendor class, those values should be used. If there are parameter values configured for the subnet the client is connected to, those should be used. The server can place its own Vendor Class identifier in the reply, so that the client can use it to decide among multiple DHCPOFFERS.

Now the DHCP server records the collected information in its local database. This "provisional lease" ensures that when the client decides to accept an offer, the information is still available, and ensures that the IP address will not be issued to another client before the first client accepts. These provisional leases need to have a time limit on them, lest clients that die between DHCPOFFER and DHCPREQUEST leave an increasing number of provisionally assigned addresses in an unusable state. This time, and the management of unaccepted provisional leases, is up to the implementor of the server.[1]

Finally, the server builds and sends a DHCPOFFER message.

---

[1] The technique of keeping a list of offered addresses and not assigning them to other clients for "a while" is not *required* by the RFC, but it is both recommended and a good idea!

Example. In response to the DHCPDISCOVER message shown in Section 4.1.3, server Z might send this DHCPOFFER packet:

op:tu:ln:hops	xid	secs flag	ciaddr
01:01:06:00	12345678	0000:8000	0.0.0.0

yiaddr	siaddr	giaddr	chaddr
10.0.2.45	0.0.0.0	0.0.0.0	01:23:45:00

chaddr (continued)			sname
01:01:00:00	00:00:00:00	00:00:00:00	00...

sname...		file....	
00...		00...	

options...			
63.82.53.63	35:01:02 33	04:00:00:01	58 36:04:10

more options...			
0.2.128 FF:00 ...			

We can see the offered address of 10.0.2.45 in the yiaddr field, the Magic Cookie in the first word of the option field, the offered lease time of ten minutes (158hex, 600 seconds) in the second option, and the server's IP address of 10.0.2.128 in the third option. The End option finishes off the packet.

5.1.3 DHCPREQUEST

Clients send DHCPREQUEST messages for four reasons:

- The client received one or more DHCPOFFERs and is choosing one of them. That is, the client is in the SELECTING state (see Figure 3-2).
- The client was in the INIT-REBOOT state and is now trying to reacquire its previous lease.
- The client was in the RENEWING state and is now negotiating an extension of its lease because T1 has expired.
- The client was in the REBINDING state because T2 expired and it is trying to either get a lease extension or a new address.

The server can distinguish these conditions by examining the client address field (ciaddr), the Server Identifier option, and the Requested IP Address option.

- If the message was sent from a client in SELECTING, the Server Identifier option will have the IP address of this server (the one the client is selecting), and the Requested IP Address option will have the IP address from the DHCPOFFER's yiaddr field.
- If the message was sent from a rebooting client, the Server Identifier option will not be present, and the Requested IP Address option will have the client's previous address.

- If the client was in the RENEWING state, `ciaddr` will have the client's current address and the Server Identifier and Requested IP Address options will not be present. The message will have been unicast to the server and the gateway address field (`giaddr`) will be zero, since the assistance of a relay agent was not necessary to forward the message

- Finally, if the client was in the REBINDING state, `ciaddr` will have an address, the Server Identifier and Requested IP Address options will not be present, and the message will have been broadcast.

The actions taken by the server depend on the inferred state of the client.

- **SELECTING.** In this case, the client is selecting from one or more DHCPOFFERs. The Server Identifier option will have the IP address of the server the client has chosen. This server will look up the provisional lease for this client, save it in the "real" lease database, and send a DHCPACK message to the client.

- **INIT-REBOOT.** In this state, the client has previously been assigned an address and wishes to confirm it for some reason; whether it is rebooting, reinitializing the network, or just feels like it. The server must make sure that the client is still on the correct network and that the IP address is correct, since the client may have been moved (perhaps it is a portable laptop computer someone has unplugged and carried to a different department). If the `giaddr` field is non-zero, then the server can tell which subnet the client is on. If the IP address the client is requesting does not match that subnet, or the address the client is requesting is not the one in the server's database, then the server should send a DHCPNAK to the client. This message should be broadcast, not unicast (either by being sent to the broadcast address on the local network, or by setting the Broadcast bit in the message so the relay agent will broadcast it), because the client's IP address may be incorrect for the network it's on and unicast packets may not arrive. If the server has never heard from this client before, then it must do nothing. The client will eventually give up and go to the INIT state and start from scratch. If the client's data is okay, and the network manager has not decided ahead of time to deny this client a renewal, then a DHCPACK message is constructed and sent.

- **RENEWING.** In this case, the client is configured and the T1 timer has expired, indicating that the lease period is at least 1/2 over. The server should check that the client's IP address (in the `ciaddr` field) is in fact the correct address for this client and is currently leased, and then it may extend the lease by sending a DHCPACK message with new T1 and T2 times. If the network manager has decided that the client's lease should not be extended, or the lease is not found in the server's database, then a

DHCPNAK should be sent. In either case, the message can be sent unicast to the `ciaddr` address.

- **REBINDING.** In this case, the client is configured and the T2 timer has expired, indicating that the lease period is at least 7/8 over. Further, the client's original DHCP server has not responded to the request when it was in the RENEWING state, so it's broadcasting in a last, desperate attempt to extend the lease. In this case, if there is more than one DHCP server in the network and it is configured so as to allow it to assign these addresses, then it can extend the lease; otherwise, it can send a DHCPNAK and have the client start over.

Example. Here is the packet server X sends back to the DHCPREQUEST of Section 4.1.5:

op:tu:ln:hops	xid	secs flag	ciaddr
02:01:06:00	12345678	0000:8000	0.0.0.0

yiaddr	siaddr	giaddr	chaddr
10.0.2.45	0.0.0.0	0.0.0.0	01:23:45:00

chaddr (continued)			sname
01:01:00:00	00:00:00:00	00:00:00:00	00...

sname...		file....	
00...		00...	

options...			
63.82.53.63	35:01:05 33	04:000000086400	36:04:10

more options...			
0.2.128 FF:00 ...			

5.1.4 DHCPDECLINE

This message means that the address sent in a DHCPOFFER was found to be in use by the client. The server must put the address on a list of unusable addresses and should notify the network manager. Finding IP addresses in use that the DHCP server thought were free probably means something is misconfigured. No server response is necessary; if the client wishes to try again, it will start over in the INIT state and send a new DHCPDISCOVER.

The server should log this event so that the network manager will know what's happening and can track down and eliminate the problem, which may be a user who has configured their computer with a static IP address from the dynamic pool, without asking if it's okay.[2]

---

[2] This does happen and makes network managers very upset; I know at least one who solves such problems with the application of wire cutters to the offending user's network cable.

5.1.5 DHCPINFORM

A DHCPINFORM message means that the client already has an IP address and just wants some parameters. The server looks up the parameters as described for the DHCPOFFER message, and sends them in a DHCPACK message unicast to the client's address (found in the `ciaddr` field). The server must not send values for T1 and T2 and should not fill in `yiaddr`; after all, the client already has an address and it isn't going to expire.

Example. If client A sent a DHCPINFORM requesting the IP address of its local router (Option 3), it might get a DHCPACK looking something like this:

op:tu:ln:hops	xid	secs flag	ciaddr
02:01:06:00	12345678	0000:8000	0.0.0.0

yiaddr	siaddr	giaddr	chaddr
0.0.0.0	0.0.0.0	0.0.0.0	01:23:45:00

chaddr (continued)			sname
01:01:00:00	00:00:00:00	00:00:00:00	00...

sname...		file....	
00...		00...	

options...			
63.82.53.63	35:01:05 03	04 10.0.1.	254 FF:00:00

more options...			
00 ...			

After the main packet header, `options` has the Magic Cookie, the DHCP Message Type (DHCPACK = 5), the Gateways option (03) of length 4 with IP address 10.0.1.254, and the address of router R on the 10.0.1.0 subnet. An End option (FF) finishes off the options field.

5.1.6 DHCPRELEASE

Polite clients will send a DHCPRELEASE message when they no longer need their assigned address. The server will mark the address as being available for use, and should save the client's address and parameters in the database in case the client connects again later. Computers with intermittent connections, like Network Computers (NCs) that get turned off when not in use and portables carried around by salespeople or field service technicians, typically take advantage of this. No server response is necessary to this message.

5.2 Expiring a Lease

There isn't a lot a server can do to force an address lease to expire. The protocol doesn't permit a DHCP server to initiate transactions, only to respond to client requests. The most aggressive thing a server can do is deny a renewal when a client requests one.

Once in a while it may be necessary for a network manager to force clients to renegotiate their leases. Perhaps the company has switched to a new Internet service provider and needs to change all their IP addresses. In this case, the best strategy is for the network manager to plan ahead. If the default lease time is usually one week, then T1 will be three and a half days. You could expect that in three and a half days all the clients will eventually ask for lease renewals, but that's a long time to wait for your network to start working again.

A better approach would be to shorten the lease time to, say, one day a week before the switch, and then to one hour a day before. This will increase the load on the server, but with T1 at thirty minutes, it will take only that long for all the clients to try to renew and get told to start over with new addresses. Some users who actually *read* the memo about the changeover may even force a new lease, either by rebooting their computer or by using whatever user interface to the DHCP client software they have available. Finally, the lease time can be pushed back to the normal time and all the users will be happy.

We'll see in Chapter 10 how the "Next Generation" IP, version 6, solves the problem with a new message type.

5.3 Static IP Assignments

Sometimes a network manager wants to have a client use the same IP address all the time, but still get the address from the DHCP server. If the manager enters a record into the lease database "by hand" for the client with the desired address, they can achieve this effect by giving the lease an "infinite" duration. In practice this means having the lease expire on the last date the computer can represent. For UNIX machines, that date is 7:14 PM, Jan 18, 2038.[3]

5.4 Summary of Fields and Options

Depending on the type of DHCP message, some fields and options are significant, and some are not. Sorting this out can be complex.

Table 5-2 presents a summary of the fields in a DHCP server message, and what should go in each field.

Table 5-3 presents the options that can go in client messages.

Following IETF usage, the terms "MAY", "MUST", "MUST NOT", "SHOULD", and "SHOULD NOT" are used in both tables to indicate whether a given field or option is required in a given message type, forbidden, merely allowed, or recommended.

---

[3] While this is effectively infinite in "Internet time", which is similar to "dog years", this date is coming faster than one might think. With 40-year mortgages becoming more popular due to higher housing costs, already mortgage amortization programs are running past this date as I write in mid-1998. Yes, the "Year 2038" problem is already rearing its head.

Table 5-2 Fields of DHCP Server Messages

Field	DHCPOFFER	DHCPACK	DHCPNAK
pop	BOOTREPLY	BOOTREPLY	BOOTREPLY
type	From "Assigned Numbers" RFC		
Helen	Hardware address length in octets		
hops	0	0	0
xid	The same xid the client sent		
secs	0	0	0
flags	Flags from client message		
ciaddr	0	ciaddr from DHCPRE-QUEST, or 0	0
yiaddr	IP address offered to client	IP address assigned to client	0
siaddr	IP address of next bootstrap server		0
giaddr	giaddr from client message		
chaddr	Hardware address from client message		
sname	Server hostname or options		Unused
file	Options or unused		
options	Options	Options	Options

Table 5-3 DHCP Server Message Options

Option	DHCPOFFER	DHCPACK	DHCPNAK
Request IP Address	MUST NOT	MUST NOT	MUST NOT
IP Address Lease Time	MUST	[a]	MUST NOT
Use file/sname Fields	MAY	MAY	MUST NOT
DHCP Message Type	DHCPOFFER	DHCPACK	DHCPNAK
Client Identifier	MUST NOT	MUST NOT	MUST NOT
Vendor Class Identifier	MAY	MAY	MAY
Server Identifier	MUST	MUST	MUST
Parameter Request List	MUST NOT	MUST NOT	MUST NOT
Message	SHOULD	SHOULD	SHOULD
Maximum Message Size	MUST NOT	MUST NOT	MUST NOT
All others	MAY	MAY	MUST NOT

[a]MUST if in response to DHCPREQUEST, MUST NOT if in response to DHCPINFORM.

5.5 Summary

This chapter covered the behavior of DHCP servers. How to assign an IP address to a client was covered in detail; address pools—the available addresses that can be assigned—must be configured first.

Next, we discussed the server's behavior for each of the messages a client can send: DHCPDISCOVER, DHCPREQUEST, DHCPDECLINE, DHCPIN-FORM, and DHCPRELEASE.

What to do when an address lease expires was the next topic, followed by how to assign static or permanent IP addresses to some clients. Finally, a summary of required and optional DHCP message fields and options was given.

DHCP Relay Agents

Why We Need Relay Agents
What Does a Relay Agent Do?

Relay agents have been mentioned in passing before now; here we'll take a look at them in detail.

6.1 Why We Need Relay Agents

DHCP clients starting from scratch have to broadcast their initial DHCPDIS-COVER messages since they don't yet know anything about the network they're attached to. Much broadcast traffic is like this; machines looking for local information and services.

Most routers are configured to not pass broadcast traffic, since a workstation in California probably doesn't need to hear about a printer in New Jersey. With over 20 million computers on the Internet today, passing broadcasts indiscriminately throughout the world would be a disaster.

Given this state of affairs, it appears that if we want to put DHCP service on a large network that is divided into a number of subnets, we would need to put a DHCP server on each subnet, so that they would be able to receive broadcast messages from any potential DHCP client.

This is not entirely acceptable to many network managers; these machines aren't free, after all, and one subnet's worth of DHCP traffic may not be heavy enough to justify an entire computer for it. The software could be installed on an existing host on the subnet, but again, it's not ideal: there may not be a suitable machine, or its owner may not want the DHCP server installed, and so on.

We can get away with fewer servers if we allow existing machines or routers to act as "relay agents", which forward messages between clients and servers.

6.2   What Does a Relay Agent Do?

A common TV or movie situation has an angry couple where the partners are not talking to each other, but instead using a child to communicate:

> "Bobby, tell your father that dinner's ready."
>
> "Dad, Mom says to tell you that dinner's ready."
>
> "Thank you Bobby. Tell your mother that I'll be there when I'm good and ready."
>
> "Mom, Dad says..."
>
> "I heard it!"

It's a cliche, but in this example, Bobby is a relay agent. He takes messages from Mom and gives them to Dad, and also takes messages from Dad and hands them to Mom.

The relay agent concept originated with BOOTP, and DHCP was designed to take advantage of the existing BOOTP relay agents. Since the agents are just shuffling the bits back and forth, they don't really need to understand the BOOTP or DHCP protocols, as long as the messages arrive safely.

The basic things that relay agents do are:

- Receive broadcast BOOTREQUEST packets and send them to a known server.
- Receive BOOTREPLY packets from the server and broadcast them on the local subnet.

The relay agent must do a little more processing itself, though; it's not just a router that forwards all packets willy-nilly (although relay agent functionality certainly can be, and sometimes is, built into routers). As far as the client on the network is concerned, it looks like the relay agent is swallowing the packets and sending replies. To the client, this is more or less indistinguishable from a real DHCP server.

The relay agent can be located in any machine, directly connected to the subnet it is serving. The relay agent can be in the router that connects the subnet to the rest of the network; this is convenient, but not necessary. A host that is not the router can still *use* the router to send the messages on to the real DHCP server.

Machines hosting relay agents can have multiple network interfaces. A router with a built-in relay agent will almost certainly have more than one interface. After all, that's what routers are *for*.

If the relay agent host has multiple interfaces, it is not required that it act as a router, and it may listen for BOOTP and DHCP requests on only a few of the interfaces. A server that is multi-homed on several subnets would make a perfectly good home for relay agents.

6.2.1 Relay Agent Configuration

Whether the relay agent is part of a router or not, it needs to know the address of the DHCP server, so that it can forward packets to the server. When the agent is set up, the network manager must configure the domain name or IP address of the DHCP server to which packets should be sent.

It is not necessary to set up relay agents on every hop between the DHCP server and the subnet being configured; only the relay agent on that subnet is necessary. Once the packet is processed by the relay agent, it is sent by normal means as a unicast packet from the agent to the server.

For example, in Figure 6-1 we see a possible configuration of an enterprise network. The subnet being managed by DHCP is on the left, with four clients and one server acting as a relay agent. The main "server farm" is on the right, with three file servers and one DHCP server. Between the server farm and our DHCP-managed subnet are three routers.

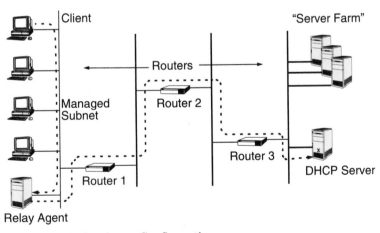

Figure 6-1 Relay Agent Configuration

When the client at the top right needs to configure itself with DHCP, it broadcasts the initial DHCPDISCOVER on the local subnet. No DCHP servers receive it, but the relay agent does. This is the first step, shown by the dotted arrow from the client down to the relay agent.

Next, since the relay agent has previously been configured with the address of the DHCP server, it sends the packet via unicast directly to that address. The normal IP routing and forwarding mechanisms operate in the three intermediate routers, and the packet arrives directly to the DHCP server.

Since the relay agent must be able to receive broadcast packets, it can operate in any of the hosts on the managed subnet, or in router 1; but, a relay agent serving this network cannot be in routers 2 or 3.

6.2.2 Processing of BOOTREQUEST

Just like a DHCP or BOOTP server, the relay agent listens for UDP packets on the BOOTP port, Port 67. Any packets on the subnet that are either broadcast or unicast to the relay agent with the destination port set to 67 will be processed by the relay agent. Packets from any legal address on the subnet will be accepted; other addresses may be rejected to protect the relay agent and the DHCP server from misconfigured or malicious data. Packets with the source IP address set to zero (0.0.0.0) are accepted too, since the client may not have an IP address yet. Indeed, since the whole point of DHCP and this relay agent is to enable a client to get an IP address, this is an essential behavior.

We now see the usefulness of the hops field. Each time the packet passes through a relay agent, the hops field is incremented, and messages arriving with a hops field that is "too large" can be discarded, as they may be the result of a "relay agent" loop. That is, one relay agent forwards the packets to a second relay agent, which forwards them to a third, which forwards them to the first, and around and around we go, with the data never coming out. To guard against this and other pathological topologies, packets with large hop counts are usually discarded. What "too large" means is a matter for the network manager to decide.

Once a packet is received by the relay agent, a little processing must be done to it. If the gateway address field (giaddr) is 0, then the packet came from the local network. The relay agent will fill in giaddr with the IP address of the interface used to receive the packet. When a reply arrives with the same giaddr, the relay agent will be able to use this field to decide which network interface to use to send the packet with. If giaddr is not zero, then it must have been filled in by another relay agent; this relay agent must leave it alone.

In no case should the broadcast address be put into the giaddr field. This will result in the server sending replies back to this address. In other words, the packets will be broadcast on the server's local subnet—almost certainly not what was intended. Since relay agents expect server replies to be unicast to them, they will not receive (or will discard) such packets.

The relay agent must now increment the hops field by one, and if UDP checksums are being used,[1] the checksum must be recalculated. Since only a few fields in the packet have been altered, one of the well-known incremental check-

---

[1] Remember, UDP checksums are optional, but a very good idea.

sum routines can be used to avoid doing the checksum over the entire packet. This is, of course, strictly a performance "hack", and should most likely only be implemented if the checksumming is found to be a performance bottleneck by actual measurements.

Finally, the message must be sent to the DHCP server, at an address configured by the network manager when the network was set up. All messages from the same client must go to the same server, so any effort on the part of the relay agent to cleverly "load balance" BOOTP and DHCP traffic against several servers must be a little more than clever; some sort of deterministic way of sending all the packets from one client to the same place. A moment's reflection on how the BOOTP and DHCP protocols work should make it clear why this is necessary. While BOOTP is a single packet exchange, imagine what would happen if a client's DHCPDISCOVER and DHCPREQUEST messages were sent to different servers.

6.2.3 Processing of BOOTREPLY Packets

Having sent the packet on toward a BOOTP or DHCP server, the relay agent will eventually receive a reply which it now needs to deal with. Relay agents listen for UDP packets from the DHCP server. When one is received, the agent will examine the `giaddr` field to determine on which network interface to transmit the message. When the relay agent sent the original DHCPDIS-COVER or DHCPREQUEST packet to the DHCP server, it filled in this field with the address of the interface on which the packet was received, so that the DHCP server would know which subnet the client's packets were coming from, and so that when the packet came back it would be able to tell which subnet to deliver it to.

If the agent only has one interface, the decision is easy, of course. If there is more than one interface, the agent must look through its list of network interfaces to find one that matches the `giaddr` field. If there's no match, the packet must be discarded.

Once the interface is chosen, other information in the packet can be used to decide how to deal with the message. If the Broadcast flag is set, the message should be sent to the IP broadcast address. The Broadcast flag is set by a client that cannot receive unicast packets until its network is fully configured. The server will set the flag in replies to this client, and the relay agent will use it.

If the broadcast address is not set, the relay agent can send the reply using unicast. From the reply, it can extract the link-layer address information from the `hlen`, `htype`, and `chaddr` fields, and send the packet directly to the client. If the Broadcast flag is not set, the relay agent is permitted to send the reply packet with a broadcast anyway. Perhaps the relay agent can't send "raw" link-layer packets due to operating system or policy limitations—however, it can still get its job done.

6.3 Summary

In this chapter, we examined the following issues surrounding DHCP relay agents:

- Why they are necessary.
- What they do exactly.
- How they are configured.
- How DHCP and BOOTP packets are processed.

CHAPTER 7

Dynamic DNS

Overview of DNS
What's the Name of My Machine?
Dynamic Updating
DDNS and Security

When you click on a link in your Web browser, it typically causes a connection to another Web server. The link contains a Uniform Resource Locator (URL) that looks something like the following:

```
http://www.prenhall.com/index.html
```

The "`www.prenhall.com`" part of the URL is the domain name of the host your Web browser should connect to. However, deep in the metaphorical salt mines of TCP/IP where the packets get assembled by the TCP/IP gnomes, the IP address of the host—the actual numbers "206.246.140.162"—need to be placed in the packet header so that the packet can be routed to the Web server.

The Domain Name System (DNS) is the distributed Internet service that provides translation from hostnames that people like to use, to the numeric addresses the TCP/IP gnomes want.

Now, if your machine has just been assigned an address by a DHCP server, what is its name?

7.1 Overview of DNS

In the old days, way back before 1984, when there were only a few hundred machines connected to the ARPANET, a simple file called HOSTS.TXT was maintained on host SRI-NIC. Every so often you'd FTP the file, install it on your computer, and you'd have a complete list of all the computers on the ARPANET. Simple and easy.

Around 1984, though, it began to be apparent that this method would soon be unworkable. The 'net was growing fast, there were nearly a thousand machines connected, and a new machine was being connected every few days![1] Updating the HOSTS.TXT file was becoming a bottleneck.

Enter the Domain Name System (DNS). This is the distributed hierarchical service for resolving names to addresses currently used in the Internet.

Each computer attached to the Internet needs a name that humans can remember. In DNS, each name is a series of components separated by periods, such as "www.prenhall.com", the Prentice Hall Web server, or "ftp.stanford.edu", the Stanford University FTP server.

The names are constructed hierarchically, rather like a tree, so that responsibility for portions of the namespace can be assigned to different organizations. These namespace parts are called "*domains*". The domain names can be read from right to left, with each portion of the domain being more specific. For example, "www.cs.stanford.edu" is the Web server in the Computer Science Department at Stanford. "edu" is the domain for "educational" organizations, "stanford.edu" is for all computers at the university, "cs.stanford.edu" is for computers in the Computer Science Department, and the last component, "www", is the actual name of the machine.

All computer names are called "domain names". Some systems allow the use of partial names. If your computer was attached to Stanford's CS network, you could probably get to the Web server with just "www". A name with additional domain components, like "www.cs", is called a "qualified domain name", and a name that includes all the domain components ("www.cs.stanford.edu") is called a "fully-qualified domain name."

The top-level domains are shown in Table 7-1. They are administered by the Internic (Internet Network Information Center), which is operated by the National Science Foundation and Network Solutions.[2] Other countries are assigned domains that start with their ISO country code. For example, the United Kingdom uses ".uk" and France uses ".fr". A national organization in each country manages name assignment there. (But, entities outside the US can get ".com" addresses, so don't assume ".com" means US, though there is a ".us" domain.)

The Internic, or another responsible organization, delegates administration of a domain to that domain's owner. So, the network managers at Prentice Hall take care of assigning names that are part of the "prenhall.com" domain, and the folks at Stanford take care of "stanford.edu". Domains can be even further

---

[1] Contrast that with today's (July 1998 is the latest data) 36.7 million hosts. Between July 1997 and July 1998, the Internet grew by some 16 million hosts, with an average of 40 hosts being connected *every minute*. Data courtesy of Network Wizards, http://www.nw.com.

[2] The administration of domain names is entering a state of flux, and this may not be accurate by the time this book is printed; the political arguments and events are, thankfully, beyond the scope of this book.

Table 7-1 Top-level Domains

Domain	Purpose
.com	Commercial organizations
.edu	Educational organizations: colleges, universities and other schools
.gov	US Government and government agencies
.net	Computers of network providers (the NIC, ISPs, etc.)
.org	Miscellaneous organizations that don't fit anywhere else
.mil	US military organizations
.int	Intended for international organizations formed by treaties, such as the United Nations or NATO

broken up and delegated. So, the Stanford folks may let the Computer Science network managers deal with the Computer Science Department domain, "cs.stanford.edu".

Now, given these hierarchically assigned and organized names, when someone types "www.prenhall.com" into their Web browser, how does the browser find out the IP address of that machine? It has to enlist the help of two entities. One is a part of the operating system called the "resolver"; its job is to "resolve" names to addresses. It does this by interacting with the other entity, the network of cooperating "name servers" that store and distribute the information about what address goes with which name.

The resolver on a given machine is configured with the address of the name server that the local network managers have decided is appropriate. When the resolver needs the IP address of "www.cs.stanford.edu", it sends a query to the name server asking, "What is the address of www.cs.stanford.edu?" The name server may know the answer, and if so, it returns the information to the resolver. If the server does not know the answer, it must ask a neighboring name server.

A set of "root servers" at the top of the hierarchy have well-known and published addresses that are usually configured into name servers, so that they can ask a root server, "What is the address of www.cs.stanford.edu?"

They will typically get a response that is the DNS equivalent of "I don't know, but this guy over here does", plus the address of the Stanford name server, one of which happens to be argus.stanford.edu[3]. Next, the query goes out to argus, who might return another "I don't know" message with a pointer to the name server in the CS Department. When that server is queried, it will return the actual address.

---

[3] In Homer's *Odyssey*, Argus was the name of Ulysses' dog. When Ulysses arrived home after 19 years of wandering, Argus recognized him, proving his identity, and promptly died. I don't *think* this story is significant in relation to Stanford's DNS servers.

The resolver and local name server will remember the address and name, and the addresses of the Stanford server and CS server, in case it needs the information later. If the information gets very old, it will eventually be discarded so that the database of locally cached information doesn't grow without bound. The time the data are kept is called the "time-to-live".

7.1.1 Organization of DNS Data

A digression on how DNS data are stored is necessary here so that the remainder of the chapter will make sense.

The portions of the DNS namespace that are handled by various servers are called "zones". All the names at Stanford University are part of the "stanford.edu" zone, delegated to them by the Internic, and those in the Computer Science Department are in the "cs.stanford.edu" zone, delegated to them by the Stanford network managers. The "stanford.edu" zone, then, contains all of the names in the "stanford.edu" domain, *except* those in "cs.stanford.edu", which have been delegated.

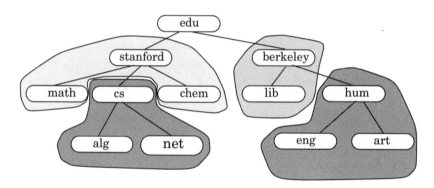

Figure 7-1 DNS Data: Domains and Zones

Figure 7-1 shows, as an example, a fictitious set of zones for a portion of the .edu namespace (everything below the names of the schools is my invention; any similarity to any real networks, living or dead, is purely coincidental). We see that the stanford.edu zone includes machines with names like "xx.stanford.edu" and also machines in the Chemistry Department, whose names are like "xxx.chem.stanford.edu". The stanford.edu zone would contain the names in the Computer Science Department, if they were not delegated to them. The cs.stanford.edu zone includes the Algorithms section and Networking section machines, as they are part of the CS Department.

Across the Bay in Berkeley, a similar situation occurs. Most of the campuses' machines lie in the berkeley.edu zone, including the Library computers. But, the Internet-savvy folks in the College of Humanities have decided to have their bit delegated to them, so they form a separate zone, including machines in hum.berkeley.edu, eng.hum.berkeley.edu and art.hum.berkeley.edu.

Notice that a zone may not extend neatly across the DNS name tree at a single level, but depends only on the delegation structure.

Each server that controls a zone maintains the DNS data in a database of "resource records". Each resource record has some information about a name in the part of the tree-like domain namespace this server is responsible for.

There are several types of resource records that can be stored in the DNS database. A few of the most common ones are described below; the format of the records shown here follows that of the disk-based files of BIND, one of the most commonly used DNS servers on the Internet.

7.1.1.1 Start of Authority (SOA)

The Start of Authority (SOA) record is of key importance to a zone. It defines the zone to other DNS servers and tells them how long the data from the zone that they have cached will be good. A typical SOA record might look like this:

```
@ IN SOA example.com. hostmaster.fnord.example.com. (
    4       ; Serial
    3600    ; Refresh
    300     ; Retry
    3600000; Expire
    3600 ) ; Minimum
```

This record starts with "@ IN SOA", indicating that this is an Internet SOA record.[4] This is followed by the name of the domain and the email address of the person responsible for the domain. This zone will consist of all names that end with "example.com" that are not delegated to other servers.

BIND's representation of the email address of the responsible person does not have an '@' in it like normal email addresses, but consists of the user part of the address, a period, and the host part. Thus, the "proper" address can be derived by replacing the first period with '@'. In the example, we would take "hostmaster.fnord.example.com", change the first period, and get "hostmaster@fnord.example.com". There are a few more similar peculiarities to the BIND file formats that I will gloss over here.

---

[4] The DNS is flexible enough to be used for data other than those relating to Internet names and addresses, but in practice tends not to be. When the Internet protocols were being developed, their staggering popularity and market success were still far in the future, so the designers tried to be cautious and flexible.

The numbers that follow are:

- The serial number, which is used by other name servers to determine when the data on the authoritative server is newer than their local copy.
- The refresh time, which is the number of seconds after which the zone should be refreshed (3600 seconds, or one hour in this example).
- The retry time, which is the number of seconds that servers should wait after a refresh fails before trying again (300 seconds, or five minutes).
- The expiration time, which is the number of seconds after which the data should no longer be considered authoritative without a refresh (3600000 seconds, 1000 hours, or nearly 42 days).
- The minimum time, which is the minimum time-to-live that should be given with each record served.

7.1.1.2 Address (A)

The main type of resource record is the address, or A-record. It looks like this:

```
www.example.com. IN  A  10.138.44.64
```

This record informs the local DNS server, and any resolvers that query it, that the name `www.example.com` should be mapped to the IP address 10.138.44.64.

7.1.1.3 Name Server (NS)

Name server records are the means by which zone delegation is accomplished. A typical NS record would look like this:

```
IN NS ns.eng.example.com
```

This indicates that the machine "`ns.eng.example.com`" is the authoritative DNS server for the Engineering Department zone at `example.com`. This record should be in the main `example.com` server so that resolvers trying to get an address in `eng.example.com` will know to ask `ns.eng.example.com` instead.

One must be careful that there is also an A-record for the delegated name server, otherwise DNS clients attempting to get the address of, say, `ns.eng.example.com` will have to send a query to `ns.eng.example.com` to get the address. And, since they don't have the address, they can't send the query.

Placing A-records for the zone's name servers in the parent zone solves this chicken-and-egg problem. These A-records are often called "glue records" since they serve to "glue" zones together.

7.1.1.4 Pointer (PTR)

Pointer records are most commonly used to implement the pseudo-domain INADDR.ARPA that maps addresses to names, the reverse of the A-record's mapping of names to addresses. Given a properly configured set of PTR and A-records, the question "What is the name that goes with this address" can be answered, as well as "What is the address that goes with this name".

A PTR record corresponding to the A-record in Section 8.1.1.3 might look like this:

```
64.44.138.10 IN PTR www.example.com.
```

Note that the octets of the address are reversed; this allows the DNS name hierarchy to be used to mimic the IP address hierarchy of nets and subnets.

7.1.1.5 Canonical Name (CNAME)

Sometimes it is convenient to have multiple names for a single host. The canonical name (CNAME) record can accomplish this. If this record:

```
alias.example.com IN CNAME realname.example.com
```

was loaded into a DNS server, then hosts could use the name "alias" to connect to realname, as well as the primary or canonical name "realname". This is very useful in creating "virtual Web hosts" for small companies; an ISP can support dozens or hundreds of virtual hosts on a single server with judicious use of CNAMEs.

7.1.1.6 Mail Exchange (MX)

A mail exchange record gives the names of machines that are willing to receive mail for a domain. For example:

```
sample.com.    IN  MX  0  postoffice.example.com.
sample.com.    IN  MX  10 mailbox.example.com.
```

tells us that to send mail to anyone at sample.com, a mail transfer program should connect instead to postoffice.example.com or mailbox.example.com. Perhaps example.com is providing this service for sample.com, or sample.com is really a "virtual domain" belonging to a division of Example, Inc. Whatever the reason, the fields are the name of the domain or host, the usual IN, 'MX' to identify the record type, the preference value (here 0), and finally, the name of the mail exchanger.

Preference values can be used to arrange multiple MX records in the preferred order of usefulness; backup maildrops can be easily arranged this way. In this example, postoffice and mailbox are both candidates for mail delivery, but postoffice will be tried first since it has the lower preference. If a connection to postoffice fails, mailbox will be tried instead.

7.1.2 Zone Transfers

Cooperating DNS servers can exchange their data in bulk by using a *zone transfer*. This is a technique that makes copies of all of the resource records of a given zone in another server, in essence preloading the cache of the other server in anticipation of future requests. This can be done either as a full transfer of the entire zone (called AXFR in DNS-jargon) or incrementally, transferring only a portion of a zone at a time (called IXFR).

7.2   What's the Name of My Machine?

So, after that quick tour of the DNS, what does it have to do with DHCP? Well, imagine your computer starts up, chats with the DHCP server, and gets an IP address to use. It initializes its network interface, and you are connected to the Internet.

How can someone else find your address? What name should they use? The DNS database needs to be updated with the name and address of this newly connected machine so that other computers can find it.

Some network managers choose not to update the DNS at all for clients which are assigned addresses by DHCP, since such clients tend to be personal computers or workstations that do not offer services to the outside world. However, there are some security-conscious sites out there that refuse connections from hosts they cannot get names for.

When a network connection is made, the other end can easily get the IP address of the other connected machine, and by using the "reverse lookup" DNS feature, they can get the name. This "reverse DNS" works just like DNS except instead of feeding in names and getting addresses, you feed in addresses and get back names.

7.3   Dynamic Updating

The original DNS system was conceived in a relatively static world. When a new host was connected, a network manager would edit the DNS database files, increment the serial number in the SOA record, and cause the DNS server to read the new files. Eventually, the zone refresh timer in other DNS servers would time out, they would see the new SOA serial number, and reload their own caches.

This is impractical in a network with DHCP; when machines are connecting at unpredictable times, with addresses that cannot be predicted in advance, a human cannot (or *will* not) keep the DNS files up-to-date. Some network managers decide that this is okay, as discussed in the previous section, but others wish to have their DNS kept up-to-date automatically.

In this section we'll discuss how DHCP and DNS servers can communicate. While several products exist that can do this, I need to point out that as I write this, these protocols are not standardized and exist only in Internet Draft form. This means they could change drastically by the time you read this. This discussion should therefore be regarded more as a report on work in progress. As of August, 1998 the current draft is "Interaction between DHCP and DNS", `draft-ietf-dhc-dhcp-dns-08.txt`, available from the usual places. (See Appendix C.)

So, assuming one wants to update the DNS when a DHCP client is assigned an address, how does it work? The DHCP client and DHCP server use the dynamic DNS updates defined in RFC2136, "Dynamic Updates in the Domain Name System (DNS UPDATE)" to send updated information to a DNS server. This RFC defines the protocol for any entity interacting with the DNS server, but not what information to update, or when.

When a DHCP server assigns an address to a client, two DNS resource records need to be updated: the A-record that maps the client's name to its newly-assigned IP address, and the PTR record that maps the IP address back to the client's name.

The DHCP server, since it "owns" the IP address, is the logical entity to update the PTR record mapping the address to a name; but, whether the DHCP client or DHCP server should do the updating is rather more controversial. One side argues that since the client knows its name, and it is the one that "cares" about the mapping, it should do the update and relieve the server of the necessity. The other view holds that allowing random clients to insert things into your DNS database is a remarkably bad idea, and that only the carefully controlled DHCP server should be permitted access to the DNS server. Both sides have some good points, and the likely resolution is to make it a configurable site policy.

7.3.1 New Option: Client FQDN (Option 81)

To allow the dynamic updating of DNS to work, there needs to be a way for the DHCP client and server to tell each other the client's fully-qualified domain name (FQDN).

A new option is introduced in this Internet Draft called the Client FQDN option, assigned option code 81. The option is formatted like other options, as is shown in Figure 7.2. The option code (81) is stored in the first byte; the length of the entire option in the second, followed by a `flags` byte and two bytes of `rcode`. The FQDN in question makes up the rest of the option.

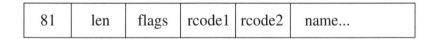

| 81 | len | flags | rcode1 | rcode2 | name... |

Figure 7-2 Client FQDN Option

The `flags` byte is used by the client to inform the server whether it wishes to update the DNS directly, or to have the server do it. The server can use the `flags` to *tell* the client which it is to be.

In a message from the client to the server, if the `flags` byte is set to 0, then the client wants to update its name's A-record with the newly assigned address. If the value is one, then it wants the DHCP server to do it. If the server sends a flags value of three, then it is telling the client it will do the update regardless of what the client sent.

The rcode bytes are used to inform the client of the DNS server's response.

7.3.2 DNS Update on the Client Side

If a client wishes to update the DNS A-record, it puts a Client FQDN option with its name into the DHCPREQUEST message, and sets the flags field to 0. Once it gets the DHCPACK, it must then proceed to do the update, of course. If the client does not wish to do the update, then it can set the flags byte of the Client FQDN option to 1. If the server does the update before it sends the DHC-PACK to the client, it will insert the code indicating the success or failure of the operation in the rcode bytes of the Client FQDN option it sends back with the DHCPACK. If the server delays the update, then it puts 255 and 0 into the bytes to indicate the update will be done shortly. Either is acceptable to the protocol and is a server implementation decision.

If a client does the A-record update and releases its address, then it should delete the A-record before sending the DHCPRELEASE to the DHCP server.

7.3.3 DNS Update on the Server Side

If the server receives a DHCPREQUEST with a Client FQDN option, and the request is acceptable, it should do the DNS A-record update. The choice of whether to do the update before or after sending the DHCPACK is up to the server implementor as mentioned above (or it could be a configurable server policy setting). The Client FQDN option should be returned in the DHCPACK, and the rcode bytes filled in as above, with either the result code from the update or the special code saying, "I haven't done that yet."

If the Client FQDN option has a one in the flags byte, then the server must do the update; if it's a zero, then the client wants to. Whether the server allows the client to is a configuration issue; if the server denies the client's wish, then it must return the Client FQDN option with a 3 in the flags byte, and the client must not do the update.

If there is no Client FQDN option in the DHCPREQUEST, but the server still determines the client's name, then the server may update the DNS A- and PTR records anyway, if so configured. If a lease expires, the server must delete the PTR record that was updated when the lease was issued; if the server did the A-record update, then that record must be deleted too. When updating, PTR records are just added, but existing A-records for a given name must be deleted before the new A-record can be added.

7.4 DDNS and Security

A number of security issues arise from the use of Dynamic DNS with DHCP. One is the problem of authentication; how can the DHCP server be sure that the entity sending it messages is authorized to do so? It is fairly easy for a programmer to cause packets with a different MAC address to be sent, so determining the identity of the client by the MAC address, while common, is not reliable.

Without security, any person who can send packets to a DNS server can alter its data, redirecting connections to other machines or rendering the network unusable. So, secure updating of DNS records is of wider interest than just usage in a DHCP context.

Ultimately, network managers must decide how much security is necessary in their installation. In a corporate campus behind a strong firewall, relatively loose constraints may be acceptable, while allowing passengers to plug random devices into a network including an aircraft's flight control and navigation computers without adequate safeguards could be disastrous.[5]

There are two parts to secure updates to the DNS. First is the DNS security scheme itself, called DNSSEC, which is described in RFC2065. Data in the DNS are authenticated with special signature (SIG) resource records that are associated with other resource records. A public-key cryptographic system is used to generate the keys and sign the records.

Next is the DNS dynamic update protocol, described in RFC2137. Using this protocol, the updater signs the new records with a private key, and the DNS server can verify, with the public key, that this entity is indeed allowed to update the DNS data.

7.4.1 Public-key Cryptography

The security of *public-key* cryptography is based on the difficulty of factoring very large numbers, which is a problem known to be computationally very difficult. In a public-key system, two numbers that are mathematically related to each other are used as *keys*. If a message is encrypted with one key, then it can be decrypted with the other and vice versa. This vice versa—the fact that the public-key system is symmetric—is important.

One of these keys is called the *private key,* and is kept secret by the person or program using cryptography; the other is called the *public key*, and is widely published for one and all to see. For instance, if Alice wants to send a message that only Bob[6] can read, then she looks up Bob's public key and encrypts her message with it. Now, only the holder of Bob's private key can decrypt it. If Bob is careful to protect his private key, then only he can do it.

If Bob wants to send a message to Alice that only Alice can read, and he wants Alice to be able to prove to herself that Bob sent it, and not some imposter,

---

[5] Don't laugh, I once saw a proposal for exactly this, despite the danger of an absurdly easy denial-of-service attack. Wiser heads prevailed, and the critical flight control systems were physically isolated from the other networks. This feature may or may not be available on newer large aircraft soon.

[6] Alice and Bob are always used in discussions of cryptography. Not being a cryptographer, I can only assume it's some kind of inside joke I don't have the right key to decode.

he does it this way. First he encrypts his message with his own private key, and then encrypts the result again with Alice's public key. When Alice receives the message, she decrypts it twice: first with her own private key, and then with Bob's public key. If she gets a comprehensible message, she can be sure it came from Bob and no one else could have read it. Two points ensure the security of the message. First, only the holder of Alice's private key—that is, Alice—can decrypt the outer layer of the message, thus assuring Bob that only Alice can read it. Second, only the holder of Bob's private key—in other words, Bob himself—could have encrypted the inner layer of the message, thus assuring Alice that only Bob could have sent it.

Digital signatures are related to this scheme. To send a digitally signed message to Bob, Alice will take the message and her private key and perform a calculation (often called a one-way hash) that yields a signature which she sends to Bob along with the message. When Bob gets the message, he can do an analogous computation with the same message, Alice's public key, and the hash or signature sent with the message. If the calculation comes out "right", then the signature is verified.

This summary is enough to make the discussion of DNSSEC understandable, but glosses over many details. How, for example, can Alice assure herself that the copy of Bob's public key she has is *really* Bob's public key and not a bogus key put on the key server by a bad guy trying to impersonate Bob? For answers to this, a good text on cryptography should be consulted.

7.4.2 KEY Resource Records

The KEY records in the DNS database match keys with DNS names. Each record contains an indication of which algorithm is used, the key itself, and some flags indicating intended usage of the key. When a record associated with the DNS name is requested, the KEY record is sent along as well.

Algorithms that can be used include MD5/RSA. RSA, Inc. has generously made available an implementation of this patented algorithm that can be used for secure DNS with no license fee, "for the good of the Internet Community".

7.4.3 SIG Resource Records

SIG records are signatures for a DNS resource record or records. The SIG record includes information about the type of record that is signed, who signed it and when, how long the signature is good, and the cryptographic signature algorithm used. Again, MD5/RSA is typical.

The records are signed with the private key that corresponds to the public key retrieved in the KEY record, so a client of the DNS server can verify the records by verifying the signature in the SIG records with that public key.

7.4.4 DNS Updates from DHCP

Now that we have KEYs and SIGs, we can see how a DHCP server generates a secure update. When installed or configured, the DHCP server needs to generate a public/private key pair and somehow transmit the public key to the DNS server it is going to update. This is usually done "by hand" by the network manager.

When the DHCP server needs to make un update to the DNS, first it assembles a set of new records for the update: typically there will be an A-record for the forward mapping of name to address and a PTR record for the reverse mapping from address to name. The DHCP server now signs the records with its private key, and sends the collection of the A-, PTR, and SIG records to the DNS server. The DNS server can now verify the signature in the SIG record, and can believe that the records came from an authorized updater.

The SIG expiration is usually set to match the lease time so that when the lease expires, so do the DNS records associated with it.

The zone serial number must be incremented when an update to the zone occurs. In an active network, this could lead to rapid spinning of the serial number, so it is permitted for it to only be incremented when a new request for the SOA record arrives. The idea is that if several updates occur between SOA requests, only the fact that the zone has changed is important, not how many updates have occurred. This allows slower growth of the serial number and a longer interval before it overflows.

7.5 Summary

This chapter covered the interaction of DHCP with the Domain Name System (DNS). After a quick review of the DNS, its concepts, and database structure, we looked at the problem of updating the DNS with the mapping of a name to a newly assigned IP address. A sketch of the protocol and new options to support it came next, followed by a discussion of the security implications of allowing dynamic updates and a review of IETF action in dealing with them.

Administering DHCP

ISC's dhcpd
Windows NT Server's DHCP Server

Knowing the theoretical principles of DHCP is all well and good, but a dose of practical reality is needed now and then. This chapter shows the details of how to perform some of the most common DHCP administrative tasks for widely used DHCP servers. The ones described are:

- dhcpd from the Internet Software Consortium (ISC) as an example of the UNIX family of servers.

- DCHP server from Windows NT Server as an example of the Windows-compatible version.

8.1 ISC's dhcpd

8.1.1 Installation

The freely distributable ISC dhcpd software runs on most UNIX systems. It is available from the ISC Web site at http://www.isc.org. It comes as a gzipped tar file, so you may need to install gzip.

dhcpd depends on the Berkeley Packet Filter (bpf), which may not be configured on your system, so that will have to be installed as well.

Create a directory to unpack and build the software in, and extract the software by running a command like the following:

```
gzip -d -c dhcp-2.0b1p16.tar.gz | tar xf -
```

You will wind up with a directory full of source files. The best approach to installation is to read the enclosed instructions, which may change slightly from release to release. The basic procedure is to run the `configure` command, inspect the generated files for correctness, and then run `make`.

Install the program in a convenient place and then create and edit the configuration file `dhcpd.conf` as described below. The configuration file allows comments, which I suggest that you use liberally as reminders to yourself and whatever other network manager may have to take over. Comments can be placed anywhere on a line in `dhcpd.conf`. They start with a "#" character and continue to the end of the line. A "#" in a quoted string does not, however, start a comment.

```
# this is a comment
option domain-name "example.com #this is not a comment"
```

Create the initial lease database by making an empty database file. This file is usually named `/var/db/dhcpd.leases`, but if your configuration is different from the default, it may be placed somewhere else.

Test the server, and once you are satisfied that it is operating properly, arrange for it to be started automatically when the system is rebooted. This will involve placing a command to start `dhcpd` in one of the system startup scripts, which live in `/etc/rc` or `/etc/rc.d`, depending on the type of UNIX.

8.1.2 Subnet Maintenance

Subnet maintenance is performed by editing the `dhcpd.conf` file. Be sure to remember to restart `dhcpd` after editing the files.

The requirement to restart the server could be viewed as awkward, especially the first time one edits the configuration and forgets to restart. There is, however, an advantage in that while you are in the middle of your changes, the server will not get confused by partially completed modifications. The model of "make changes, then tell the server to read them" does tend to prevent this kind of problem.

I would strongly recommend, as a matter of general principal, that you keep all the configuration files in a version control system like SCCS, RCS, or CVS. If your installation is a large one, with a team of administrators, it might be wise to have a policy that the last-checked-in version of the configuration files is the one that's used, and that any changes that are not properly checked in with a reasonable explanation of the changes will disappear without notice. Few things are more frustrating than finding that the configuration of a server was changed in an unknown way by an unknown person some time in the past, and when the power fails it will no longer boot properly.

8.1.2.1 Defining a Subnet

To have dhcpd manage addresses on a given subnet, place a subnet command in the dhcpd.conf file. To have it manage the addresses in the 10.0.10 subnet of our sample network, these lines would work:

```
subnet 10.0.1.0 netmask 255.255.255.0 {
    range 10.0.1.32 10.0.1.64;
}
```

To manage more than one range of addresses, just add additional range commands:

```
subnet 10.0.1.0 netmask 255.255.255.0 {
    range 10.0.1.32 10.0.1.64;
    range 10.0.1.75 10.0.1.89;
}
```

8.1.2.2 Changing or Deleting a Subnet

To change or delete a subnet is quite simple: Edit dhcpd.conf. Delete the subnet you wish to disappear, or alter an existing subnet, save the file, and restart dhcpd.

8.1.3 Lease Maintenance

dhcpd keeps its database of lease information in a text file, usually named /var/db/dhcpd.leases. Whenever a lease changes state (i.e., it is granted, released, or renewed), a line is appended to this file.

Periodically (on the first lease change after 1000 leases, or after an hour), the lease database is rewritten so that the file doesn't grow to fill the entire disk. If the server should crash during this process, there is a possibility that the old file may have been moved but the new file is not yet written; in this case, it is better to restore the old file (named /var/db/dhcpd.leases~) than to create a new database file; the latter action would cause the loss of all extant bindings, and as noted in the manual, "chaos will ensue".

If instead the old file is restored, only the record of the last change will be lost, or perhaps no changes will be lost if the rewrite was triggered by the timer. In either case, restore the old file by renaming it as /var/db/dhcpd.leases before starting the DHCP server.

8.1.3.1 Examining Leases

Since leases are always immediately written to the leases file, /var/db/dhcpd.leases, examining a lease is as simple as finding the last mention of it in the file.

A lease looks like this:

```
lease 10.0.1.32 {
    starts 6 1998/08/15 22:53:05;
    ends 0 1998/08/16 22:53:05;
    hardware ethernet 01:23:45:00:01:01;
}
```

Here we see that the lease entry starts with the keyword "lease", and is followed by the assigned IP address. Next, inside the curly braces, come various bits of information about the lease. This example is pretty minimal; it has only the start and end time of the lease, and the hardware address.

This lease starts on Saturday, the 15th of August, 1998 at 22:53:05 GMT. The first number is the day of the week, with Sunday being 0, Monday 1, and so on. The rest of the time specification is year/month/day hour:minute:second. The lease expires one day (86,400 seconds) later, on Sunday. The hardware address of this client is an Ethernet address, with the value 01:23:45:00:01:01.

8.1.3.2 Changing or Deleting Leases

Changing or deleting a lease "by hand" with the ISC dhcpd is a bit awkward. First, kill the server by sending a SIGTERM (the default signal sent by the UNIX kill command) to the dhcpd process. The process ID can be found in the file /var/run/dhcpd.pid. Next, edit the dhcpd.leases file to change or delete existing leases as desired. Be sure to make a copy of the file before you change it, just in case. Finally, restart the dhcpd program, and it will read the newly-tweaked lease database and believe your changes as the absolute truth.

8.1.4 Static IP Assignments

To make a permanent assignment of a DHCP-managed address to a client (so that it will get its address with DHCP, but always get the same one, guaranteed), use the fixed-address command in the configuration file. It can be used in a host directive to assign a permanent address to a client.

```
host david.example.com {
    fixed-address 10.0.2.1;  # always give david this addr
    hardware ethernet 01:23:45:00:02:01; # his ethernet addr
}
```

The hardware command must be present, of course, since that is how dhcpd will recognize the machine that gets this address.

8.1.5 Client Parameters and Options

Client parameters are assigned with commands in the configuration files. Globally applicable parameters can be placed at the beginning of the file, before any subnet commands. If the parameters are specific to a subnet, they can be placed within the subnet, before the range statements. Finally, groups of hosts can be created with a group command, and they can be given group-specific parameters.

For example, a complete configuration file for our sample network might look like this:

```
option domain-name "example.com"
option domain-name-servers xavier.example.com

 subnet 10.0.1.0 {
    option routers 10.0.1.254
    option subnet-mask 255.255.255.0;
    default-lease-time 3600;    # one hour
    max-lease-time 86400;       # one day
    range 10.0.1.32 10.1.0.64
 }

subnet 10.0.2.0 {
    option routers 10.0.2.254
    option subnet-mask 255.255.255.0;
    default-lease-time 7200;    # two hours on this subnet
    max-lease-time 43200;       # 12 hours
    range 10.0.2.32 10.2.0.64
 }

# Give this portable fixed addresses on each subnet.
host david.example.com {
    fixed-address 10.0.1.4;
    fixed-address 10.0.2.1;
    hardware ethernet 01:23:45:00:02:01; # his ethernet addr
 }
```

A complete list of options supported by the ISC DHCP server is given in the manual page dhcp-options, which comes with the package.

8.1.6 Reporting

ISC's dhcpd doesn't come with any tools for generating reports, like lists of leases about to expire, or subnets that are close to getting full. However, since all the information is contained in an up-to-date text file, it should be straightforward to write simple awk or perl scripts to extract and summarize data.

8.1.7 Backing Up the DHCP Databases

Again, since the data is in plain text files, making a backup of the DHCP database is a simple matter of making a copy of the data files in a safe place. Be sure to make copies of the configuration files as well as the database.

8.1.8 Getting More Information

The ISC DHCP server is not a commercial product, being produced and distributed "for the good of the community" by dedicated volunteers. ISC offers support contracts for a fee, and there are several Internet mailing lists that allow users of the software to exchange tips, tricks, and tales of woe.

You can subscribe to the mailing lists by visiting

```
http://www.fugue.com/dhcp/lists
```

and filling out the simple form. Three lists are maintained there:

- **dhcp-announce.** Announcements relating to ISC and their DHCP server software: new releases and so on.

- **dhcp-server.** Users of the ISC DHCP server discuss installing, running, and maintaining the server. Folks exchange problems and solutions.

- **dhcp-client.** Users of the ISC DHCP client software discuss installing and running it, problems they are having, and how they solve them.

8.2   Windows NT Server's DHCP Server

The Windows NT system comes with a DHCP server. The DHCP server comes with a management tool called the DHCP Manager (dhcpadmn.exe). The DHCP Manager can manage several NT DHCP servers at once. Add servers to the manager with the menu item Server->Add. Figure 8-1 shows the simplest case: managing one server that is running on the same machine as the management application.

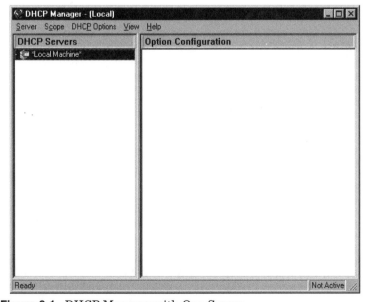

Figure 8-1   DHCP Manager with One Server

8.2.1 Vocabulary

The Microsoft DHCP server uses a unique term: *scope*. A scope, in Microsoft lingo, is a set of addresses that a given server can assign. A scope is a contiguous block of addresses in a single subnet. Sub-ranges of addresses can be excluded from a large scope. Scopes have names, and a server can handle multiple scopes

Client parameters can be assigned to a scope, so that they will be supplied to any client that is granted an IP address from that scope.

If Windows NT Service Pack 2 (or higher) is installed, then a feature called a *superscope* is added. This allows scopes to be aggregated into larger units, which can be assigned parameters as a group.

Static or fixed assignments of addresses are called *reservations*.

8.2.2 Installation

The Microsoft DHCP server is not installed by default, so it must be installed before it will operate. Open the Network icon from the Control Panel and select the TCP/IP Installation Options dialog. There will be a choice labelled "DHCP Server Service"; select it and the server will be loaded.[1]

It installs as a "service", so it is started automatically when Windows NT boots.

8.2.3 Subnet Maintenance

Subnets—really scopes—are created through the DHCP Manager tool. Scopes are created with the Scope->Create menu item, which brings up a Scope Properties window, as seen in Figure 8-2, where we are defining a scope for the 10.0.1.0 subnet of the sample network.

IP addresses to be managed by DHCP should be added to the scope. The best approach is to put the lowest and highest addresses in the Start Address and End Address fields, respectively, and use the Excluded Addresses feature to exclude any addresses within the range that are not to be managed. Note that this is different from the ISC approach, wherein multiple ranges of addresses can be configured; here it is one big range with bits blocked out. Note that both single addresses and ranges of addresses can be excluded. Also on the Scope Properties window are entries for the subnet mask, lease duration and scope name, and a comment.

A scope must be *activated* with the Scope->Activate menu before DHCP will begin managing it. Figure 8-3 shows the main DHCP Manager window after two scopes for our sample network have been defined. In this window, subnet1 has been activated, which is indicated by the little rays of light emanating from the lightbulb; on a color screen, the lightbulb changes from dull white to yellow when a scope is activated.

---

[1] But, where is it loaded *from*? There is a folder under the System folder that contains a set of ".CAB" files that contain drivers, services, and other stuff that can be installed after the system is set up. If it's not there, you will have to use the original NT CD-ROM.

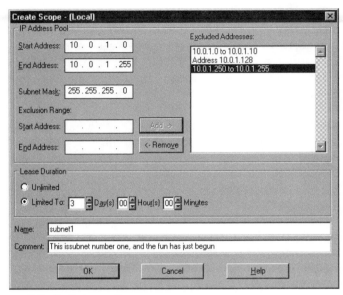

Figure 8-2 Defining a Scope

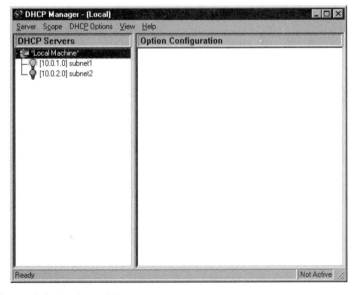

Figure 8-3 Activated Scopes

8.2.4 Lease Maintenance

Leases can be examined and manipulated with the Scope->Active Leases menu item, which brings up a window with a list of active leases (see Figure 8-4).

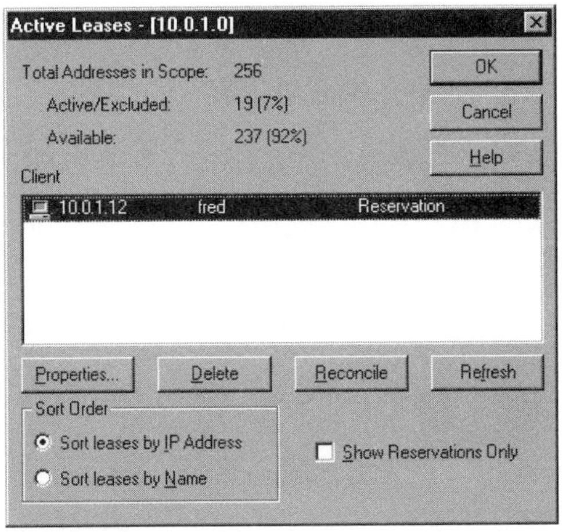

Figure 8-4 Lease Manipulation

The listing shows the IP address, name, and type of lease in a scrolling window, which can be sorted by name or IP address. The parameters issued to the client can be viewed and edited with the Properties button. Leases can be deleted with the Delete button.

8.2.5 Static IP Assignments

The DHCP Manager menu item Scope->Add Reservation lets you assign a specific IP address to a client. Clients are specified by the hardware or MAC address and host name, as seen in Figure 8-5.

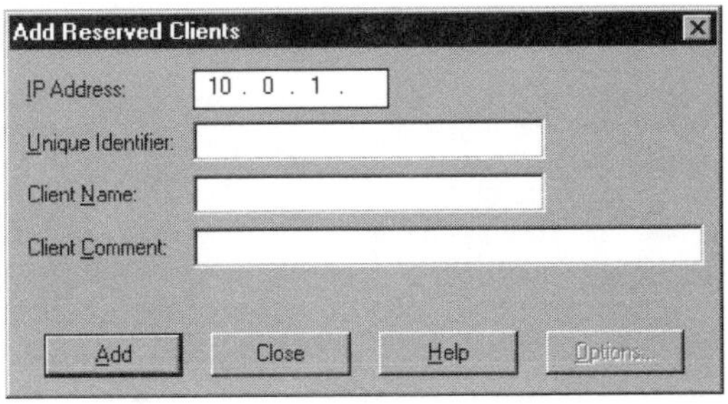

Figure 8-5 Static IP Address Assignment

8.2.6 Client Parameters and Options

Parameters and options can be assigned to scopes with the DHCP Options menu of the DHCP Manager. The dialog shown in Figure 8-6 allows you to scan the list of supported options, select which ones to set for this scope, and enter their values.

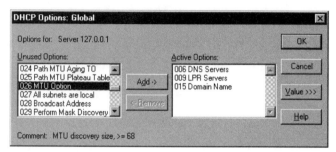

Figure 8-6 Selecting Options

Options can be set globally, applying to all scopes, specified for a given scope, or a set of default options to be assigned to new scopes can be created. The option value editing windows vary according to the type of data required for the option. Figure 8-7 shows the window used for editing an array of IP addresses, which is one of the most common data types used, for example, for most servers a client might be interested in.

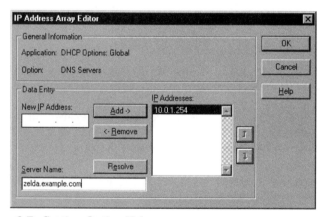

Figure 8-7 Setting Option Values

8.2.7 DHCP and the Registry

There are a large number of items related to DHCP in the Registry (Figure 8-8), most of which should probably not be manipulated "by hand". For example, each possible option has a Registry entry with information about the option code, the option name, and a description and its data format. The keys are kept in `HKEY_LOCAL_MACHINE\System\CurrentControlSet\Services\DHCP Server`.

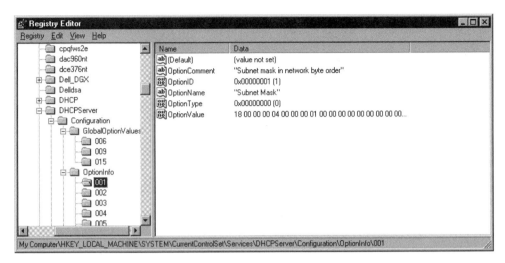

Figure 8-8 DHCP Options in the Registry

8.2.8 Backing Up the DHCP Databases

The Microsoft DHCP server has an integrated backup feature. Periodically, the data files are copied to a backup folder. The location of the backup
folder and the backup interval (which defaults to once per hour) can be set with
Registry keys in `HKEY_LOCAL_MACHINE\System\CurrentControlSet\Ser-`
`vices\DHCP Server\Parameters` as shown in Figure 8-9.

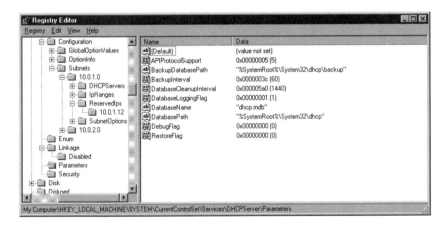

Figure 8-9 DHCP Backup Parameters

8.3 Summary

In this chapter, we saw the ways that common administrative tasks, like defining subnets, assigning option values, and manipulating leases, can be done in
the ISC DHCP server and the Windows NT DHCP Server.

Lightweight Directory Access Protocol (LDAP) and DHCP

What Is LDAP?

Integrating LDAP and DHCP

With the growth of directory services on the Internet, many organizations are looking toward integrating their DHCP service with some sort of directory, so that administration of diverse functions can be done with a common tool. The most commonly proposed directory service is the IETF's simplified version of X.500, LDAP.

LDAP is a standard, vendor-neutral, open protocol. Implementations abound for most common platforms and interoperability between independent implementations is well-tested. It's therefore well-suited for use in the Internet.

9.1   What Is LDAP?

The Lightweight Directory Access Protocol (LDAP) is a simplified version of the OSI Directory Access Protocol (DAP), also known by its standard number, X.500. Where X.500 suffers from the same "design-by-committee" that has slowed acceptance[1] of the rest of the OSI protocol suite, LDAP has been stripped down to the parts that people actually use, and operates with the TCP/IP protocols instead. Some X.500 features that turned out not to be used very much were left out, and the packet encoding was simplified. There are a number of commercial and freely distributable implementations of both LDAP servers and clients.

A "directory", in this sense, is a kind of database that allows the association of data with a unique identifier, or "name". The DNS described in Chapter 7 can

---

[1] In other words, OSI is pretty much dead and TCP/IP has "won", an eventuality not surprising to most folks who have to implement protocols instead of attend committee meetings.

be considered to be a directory; using the name of a computer, you can search the directory for the IP address that is assigned to it.

LDAP is designed to be a distributed protocol, with sub-directories arranged as trees. Individual servers can provide portions of the directory tree, handing off requests up and down the branches as necessary.

Following the OSI's internationally flavored scheme, the level below the top level, or "root" node, consists of nodes representing *countries*. Each country has sub-nodes that represent *organizations*, and each organization has sub-nodes that represent *organizational units*. The nodes under an organizational unit represent *individuals*: computers, printers, or even people. Each individual node can then have data associated with it: address, phone number, eye color, IP address, favorite chocolate bar, whatever you like.

Once the data are stored in the directory, they can be retrieved with queries. This is not, however, a relational database. Queries like "What is Berry's favorite chocolate?" or "What is his phone number?" are easy; more complex queries that are simple for a relational database, like "Who are all the male programmers in the 94303 zip code who have blue eyes and IP addresses in the 10.0.0.0 network?" are much harder, requiring the client to enumerate the individuals in a node or perhaps several nodes, and check to see if they match the query.

This is okay, since LDAP is not *supposed* to be a general-purpose database. The search and query facilities are adequate for a directory. After all, you don't expect to pick up the Los Angeles phone directory and easily answer the question "Who are all the people named 'Jim' who have phone numbers divisible by 7?"

LDAP doesn't have the complicated transaction models with multi-phase commit and rollback that relational databases use, either.

LDAP is specified by the IETF, and the current version number is 3. The RFCs describing LDAP in detail (RFC2251 through RFC2256) are available from the usual places (see Appendix B).

Major new features in version 3 include:

- **Referral.** Data can have attributes called "refs" that can allow distributed representation of information. Data stored in one server can be "included" by reference in another.

- **Security.** LDAP transactions can be authenticated (the server and client prove their identities to one another) and secured (no one else can see what they're talking about) using either the Simple Authentication and Security Layer (SASL, in RFC 2222) or the Transport Layer Security protocol, which is still in draft status.

- **Unicode.** Data in directory entries can use the Unicode character set, so that names like François, Håkon, and Nguyên can be easily represented.

- **Extensibility.** A mechanism for easily incorporating extensions into LDAP is provided. Proposals for extensions like dynamic directory services, language codes, added security, and server-side sorting of results can be found in any Internet Drafts repository.

9.1.1 **LDAP Database Organization**

The "things" that are stored in an LDAP database are called *objects*, or *entries*. Each object has a *type*, or *class*, which tells what kind of object it is, and *attributes*, which are the properties of the object.

An attribute also has a type; in addition, it has a *syntax*, which tells how the data in the attribute are to be interpreted (string? number? time? IP address?), and one or more *values*. The LDAP Standard provides a number of standard types and syntaxes for use in building objects.

The attributes of an object are divided into two types: required and optional (or, MUST and MAY). The required attributes are ones that must be present in every object of this type; the optional ones may or may not be there. This allows flexibility in building the database.

Each object type is assigned a unique hierarchical identifier called an Object Identifier (OID). These OIDs are assigned exactly like the OIDs for SNMP objects. The hierarchy of OIDs is not related to the LDAP data hierarchy; it's arranged more by the organization issuing the identifiers.

Each object has a name, and the name of an object is kept in one of its attributes, the Distinguished Name (DN). Any LDAP object can be completely identified by enumerating the names of all the nodes in the tree, from the root to the object in question; the collection of these names is called the *fully-qualified* Distinguished Name.

Data in LDAP directories is organized according to a plan or *schema*, which describes what objects are present (and possibly defines new ones) and how they are organized. Armed with the schema, a client can ask intelligent questions of the LDAP server.

When a client asks the LDAP server for information, it must supply three pieces of information:

- **A base DN.** The location in the tree where the search should start.
- **A filter.** A list of attributes to examine, values desired for them, and criteria deciding if an object matches the query.
- **A scope.** How much to limit the search: Should only the object named by the base DN be examined? Or, shall we examine all objects that are children of this object, or traverse the entire sub-tree rooted here?

The server will then look for the information and return what it finds to the client.

9.1.2 **More Information**

A good resource for information about LDAP is kept at the Innosoft Corporation Web page:

```
http://www3.innosoft.com/ldapworld/index.html
```

And of course, the RFCs should always be consulted.

9.2 Integrating LDAP and DHCP

At this point, one may wonder why anyone would contemplate integrating DHCP with LDAP. The answer, as with many issues in today's Internet, turns out not to be related to the DHCP mechanism at all, but more to the *management* of DHCP.

Using LDAP as a back-end database and configuration store for DHCP has several benefits. LDAP is scalable by design, so that the DHCP system implemented using it will be as well (even if individual servers are not). It will therefore serve large, perhaps geographically (or networkologically) dispersed organizations, like global corporations and large universities. The use of a unified storage format for all DHCP addresses, configuration, and leases will lead to easier management. The drawbacks are that the LDAP/DHCP scheme is more complex, with more points of failure, and is not yet fully standardized.

There are two primary proposals for connecting DHCP with LDAP: Microsoft's Directory Enabled Networking (DEN) and an IETF Internet Draft sponsored by T. Miller et. al. from Novell (`draft-miller-dhcp-ldap-schema-00.txt` is the name in the Drafts repositories).

In both schemes, the DHCP server is a client, at least conceptually, of the LDAP server. (As an implementation detail, the two servers could be part of the same program.) The DHCP server will take its configuration information from the LDAP database, replacing or enhancing existing configuration methods, and will post updates and changes to the LDAP server, so that they can be viewed by interested (and authorized) parties.

9.2.1 Microsoft's DEN

Microsoft's DHCP service for DEN is oriented toward providing uniform and centrally administered DHCP for an enterprise: a large company or a university campus, for instance. The design goals include:

- Global configuration.
- Authorization and enumeration.
- Server grouping.
- Multiple views.
- Server replacement.
- Error checking.
- Site integration (not defined).
- Templates (not defined).

The Microsoft proposal establishes five new DHCP objects:

- **DHCP Base class.** The basic class from which others are derived.
- **DHCP Root.** Holds global configuration information and a list of DHCP Server objects in the enterprise.
- **DHCP Server.** A class representing an actual computer providing DHCP service.
- **DHCP Subnet.** A class representing a subnet managed by DHCP.
- **DHCP Reservation.** Microsoft's term for a DHCP binding or association between a DHCP client and an IP address.

There should be one Root object defined for a given enterprise network. This object will provide a uniquely named place to start looking at the DHCP service. It also has global configuration parameters: the default values for the enterprise network. Finally, a list of references to DHCP servers in the enterprise is provided.

Each server is represented by a DHCP Server LDAP object. It contains a list of references to DHCP Subnet LDAP objects representing the subnets that the server manages.

The Subnet object contains the information about the subnet: the IP address of the network, the subnet mask, and a list of ranges of IP addresses. There can also be a list of references to Reservations, which include the IP and hardware addresses, client name, and lease time information.

LDAP-based management tools can change the parameters and configurations of the DHCP system. The DHCP servers then "publish" the new reservations by creating the appropriate Reservation objects. Observing the state of the network becomes a simple matter of traversing the tree of LDAP objects and building an informative report.

9.2.2 IETF Draft Proposal

First off, while I write this book, the IETF proposal is still an Internet Draft. I need to make it clear that it is therefore a "work in progress", and there is no guarantee that it will become a standard in the future.

The draft IETF proposal establishes several new LDAP objects:

- **DNS/DHCP locator.** The locator holds the DNs of DNS and DHCP objects in the enterprise system. This allows these objects to be found without a possibly extensive search of the LDAP tree structure. Also stored in the locator is global configuration information that applies to all nodes underneath.
- **Subnet.** The subnet object, in addition to the required subnet address and address mask, can also contain configuration attributes for the addresses it

manages, which may be different from those assigned globally. For example, if a given subnet needs a special domain name, this is the place to put it.

- **Subnet address range.** These children of the subnet object represent addresses that are part of the subnet, and indicate whether this range is to be included in the set of managed addresses or excluded. As usual, configuration options can be placed here.
- **IP address.** This object represents an IP address that can be assigned to a client; if it is assigned, it will contain the lease information: lease time, when granted, hardware address, and DHCP options. These objects can be created by the DHCP server when a lease is granted, or by the network manager.
- **Subnet pool.** This object groups subnets together so that subnets serviced by a given relay agent can be managed by a single server.
- **DHCP server.** This object describes a DHCP server, and provides configuration information for the server, such as site policies. It includes preliminary information to support server redundancy or "fail-over", whereby one server can take over from another that fails in some way. (Fail-over is discussed more in Chapter 11.)

9.3 Summary

LDAP, the "kinder, gentler" X.500 directory protocol, is becoming increasingly interesting for DHCP vendors to provide scalable distributed access to and management of DHCP information.

While the Microsoft and IETF schemes for integrating LDAP and DHCP seem to be different in detail, close examination reveals that they are similar in spirit. Both have a top-level object with enterprise-wide information, and objects representing servers, subnets, and clients.

As both proposals work their way toward standardization, it is to be hoped that they converge on a useful DHCP schema that can satisfy, or at least minimally annoy, both camps.

IP Version 6 and DHCP

Overview of IPv6
IPv6 and DHCP

The "Next Generation" version of the IP protocol is Version 6 (the current version in wide use on the Internet is Version 4). IPv6 was developed in large part to deal with the problem that IP addresses are seen to be running out. The explosive exponential growth of the Internet is showing no signs of slowing down yet (though like all exponential growth processes in a medium with limited resources, it *will* slow down eventually—if nothing else, when the entire mass of the galaxy is converted into computers, it will be hard to grow further). Since the Version 4 IP address is only 32 bits long, no more than about four billion addresses can exist. Since the address space is not allocated densely (i.e., there are unused ranges of addresses), some pessimists fear the end may come in a few years.

Besides a larger address space, many folks in the network community saw the design of the new protocol as an opportunity to build in some of the advances in networking technology developed in the nearly twenty years since IPv4 was deployed.

10.1 Overview of IPv6

The main motivation for the development of IPv6 was, of course, growth of the Internet. Not only was the address space getting increasingly fragmented and scarce, but the tables in core Internet routers were (and are!) getting very large.

So far, router manufacturers have been able to keep up with the growth, but many Internet engineers would breath a sigh of relief if improved routing algorithms were deployed. If the growth were to accelerate, things could get dicey.

Alas, it looks like growth *will* accelerate. Some the things that may cause this are:

- Increased use of mobile networked devices, such as Palm Pilots with radio modems, which are already being marketed.
- Wireless telephones with network interfaces. At least one digital wireless phone comes with a built-in WWW browser!
- Entertainment devices, like network addressable set-top boxes or even televisions capable of fetching on-demand video streams from distributed video servers.

All of these examples are large markets that have previously not needed network addresses of any public kind. As they and similar devices join the Internet, there is a distinct possibility that growth will increase past current projections.

The key features of IPv6 are described below.

10.1.1 Addressing

IPv6 addresses are 128 bits long, which is an enormous number. This large an address allows 340,282,366,920,938,463,463,374,607,431,768,211,456 distinct addresses. If these addresses were uniformly assigned about the earth, we could have 66,557,079,334,886,694,389 per square centimeter.

It is not expected, of course, that these addresses be assigned uniformly. What this truly enormous address space allows for is for various hierarchical addressing schemes to be used without fear of running out.

A section of the address space is reserved for multicast, link-local, and site-local addresses. Multicast addresses correspond to multicast groups; collections of machines that receive all the packets sent to that multicast address. This technique is not only useful in such applications as video-conferencing, but in various infrastructure operations, as we'll see later. It allows only nodes that are "interested" in a given type of traffic to receive it. Nodes that are not routers do not need to process router discovery packets; for instance, the packets can be discarded at a very low level, perhaps by the network interface itself. Multicast is not optional as it is in IPv4; it is required to be implemented in all IPv6 hosts.

Local use addresses only have significance in a local area. Link-local addresses are restricted to a given network link or segment; site-local addresses have significance only in a given site. They are made up by assembling the appropriate link-local or site-local prefix, the subnet ID (for site-local addresses), and the network interface ID. In the case of an Ethernet, the interface ID would be the MAC address of the interface.

Local use addresses allow systems and even entire companies to begin local operations before receiving assigned addresses. Consequently, they do not have to worry about renumbering everything when it happens. They also simplify initialization procedures, since a booting system can use a link-local address to communicate with local servers as a full peer, eliminating the pesky chicken-and-egg problems prevalent in IPv4 installations.

10.1.2 Packet Format

The IPv6 packet header is much simpler than the IPv4 header, even though it is bigger. Of course, since the IPv4 header is 20 octets (or 160 bits) and two IPv6 addresses (source and destination) total 256 bits, this is hardly surprising.

Version	Priority	Flow Label		
Payload Length			Next Header	Hop Limit
Source Address (128 bits)				
Destination Address (128 bits)				

Figure 10-1 IPv6 Packet Header Format

The packet format is shown in Figure 10-1. The Version field is, of course, coded with 6. The Priority field lets the sender of the packet identify what it thinks the priority of the packet is. This is intended to aid in the control of congestion; packets with higher priority will be let through, while lower priority ones may be delayed, or dropped altogether.

The Flow Label field allows packets belonging to a particular stream of information, or *flow*, to be labelled with a unique identifier. Exact usage of this field is yet to be completely established, but it will be useful in providing guaranteed quality-of-service connections, which IPv4 lacks completely.

The Payload length gives the length of data following the header, and the Next Header field identifies the type of the header after this one—there can be multiple headers serving different purposes, much as TCP packets on an Ethernet have Ethernet, IP and TCP headers all in the same frame.

The Next Header field is also used to implement IPv6 options, additional features not needed in every packet. A special header for each option is specified and is included after the IPv6 header proper.

10.1.3 Authentication and Privacy

Authentication and privacy were seen as very important by the protocol designers, and they were incorporated into the design as required features.

Authentication is provided by an extension header that provides cryptographic authentication of the source of the packets; this could help prevent many attacks on networks. One could be sure, for instance, that this routing table update packet really came from the neighboring router and hasn't been tampered with *en route*.

A similar scheme is used for privacy; the contents of the packet can be encrypted, with an extension header providing the necessary information (apart from the actual encryption key) for the other end to decrypt.

Both schemes are designed to be flexible, so that new algorithms can be incorporated as necessary.

10.1.4 Automatic Configuration

IPv6 provides a mechanism for hosts to configure their IP addresses, seemingly eliminating the need for DHCP (but see below; it's not completely unnecessary). The Neighbor Discovery (ND) protocol allows IPv6 hosts to invent a link-local IP address from their hardware address (or other unique identifier). To make sure it's an unused address, a message should be sent to it; no reply means the address is not in use.

Once they have a valid IP address, the host can look for IPv6 routers with a router solicitation message using multicast. All IPv6 routers will be listening to the all-routers multicast address, listening for such messages, and replying with router advertisement messages. This use of multicast allows "maintenance" packets to be sent only to machines that need them, as well as reducing duplicated packets over inter-network links.

Using the address prefix in the advertisement message, the host can create a globally valid address it can use in the Internet.

Network managers who have had to go through the trials and tribulations of renumbering a local network because of a change in Internet service providers will appreciate this; all one needs is to merely reconfigure the routers with the new addresses, and all the hosts will autoconfigure with the new addresses next time they boot. Arranging for all the hosts to boot is left as an exercise; I don't recommend using the main circuit breakers for the building. (Seriously, a memo saying "reboot your PC Monday or you won't be able to use the "net" should suffice. Well, in an ideal world it would.)

10.1.5 More Information

This is only the briefest summary of IPv6 needed to understand the following sections; for more information, consult the books listed in the Bibliography, or visit the World Wide Web. Perhaps the best place to start would be:

```
http://playground.sun.com/pub/ipng/html/ipng-main.html
```

10.2 IPv6 and DHCP

Given the autoconfiguration described in Section 10.1.4, why would we need DHCP with IPv6 at all? There are reasons:

- Some network media don't support the multicast protocols needed for auto-configuration: point-to-point links and non-broadcast multiple-access (NBMA) technologies such as ATM and frame relay.
- Some small networks could be set up without a router, which is necessary for IPv6 autoconfiguration.
- A network manager may wish to control and assign configuration parameters not supported by the autoconfiguration protocols.

So, DHCP for IPv6 (DHCPv6) isn't as useless as it might seem at first glance. Since DHCPv6 is also a work in progress (the packet formats were changed at the last IETF I attended, for instance), I won't give a bit-level description of the protocol, but settle for a high-level description and suggest you consult the current Drafts for details.

One feature of IPv6 is the lack of BOOTP support; since other mechanisms exist to provide the equivalent service and there is no base of legacy equipment to deal with, it has been discarded. Additionally, many of the currently defined DHCP options are unnecessary in IPv6, since the Neighbor Discovery protocol or Service Location protocol[1] provide information about routers and so on.

DHCP servers and relay agents are required to join the link-local All-DHCP-Agents multicast group, all servers must join the site-local All-DHCP-Servers group, and all relay agents must join the site-local All-DHCP-Relays group. Servers and agents transmit to UDP Port 546; clients transmit to UDP Port 547.

Six message types are defined for DHCPv6. The packet formats are different from DHCP for IPv4, so I won't go into full detail since they may change again soon. One nice feature of the current formats that is unlikely to change is that the message-type byte comes first in the packet; it isn't buried in the options field by BOOTP compatibility.

10.2.1 DHCP Solicit Message

A new feature in DHCPv6 is the DHCP solicit message. A client trying to configure an interface sends this message to the All-DHCP-Agents multicast address in hopes of getting replies with the addresses of DHCP servers. If there is no DHCP server on the local link, but there is a relay agent, then the relay agent will forward the message to the All-DHCP-Servers multicast address, and forward the servers' replies to the client.

---

[1] See RFC2165, "Service Location Protocol".

10.2.2 DHCP Advertise Message

The DHCP servers willing to service a client each send back a DHCP Advertise message to so inform the client. The Advertise message may contain the unicast IP address of the server, in which case the client will use that address for further communication. The message may also contain a server preference field, which contains a number indicating the server's "willingness" to service the client. If a client gets multiple advertisements, then it should pick the server to use based on this field.

10.2.3 DHCP Request Message

The client can ask for configuration parameters with a DHCP Request message. It must already "know" of a server address obtained with the Solicit/Advertise messages.

The information the client wishes to receive is requested with extensions defined in another document. This allows a uniform mechanism for extending the protocol, and the extensions are not limited by the size of existing fields as in the IPv4 option scheme.

Extensions defined in the DHCPv6 Extensions Draft so far include:

- **IP address.** The client can request a specific IP address, a preferred lifetime for the address, or a desired DNS name.
- **Time offset and time zone.** These are two ways of determining the client's offset from Coordinated Universal Time (UTC, commonly but slightly incorrectly known as GMT). The offset in seconds from UTC or the POSIX time zone string can be supplied.
- **Domain name server.** A client can request and receive a list of DNS server addresses.
- **Domain name.** The default domain name that should be used by the client.
- **Directory agent.** The address of a directory agent used by the Service Location Protocol (SLP).
- **Service scope.** If the client is a service agent, the scope it should use for SLP requests is here.
- **Network time protocol server.** The addresses of NTP servers.
- **NIS and NIS+ information.** The default domain and server addresses for both NIS and NIS+.
- **Vendor-specific information.** Certain clients may wish to be provided special information relevant only to equipment made by their vendor, or specific to a given class of machine. Network computers, cable modems, and X-terminals are examples.
- **TCP keepalive interval.** Most TCP implementations can send a periodic message to keep TCP connections open; this extension specifies the interval between these messages.

- **Maximum DHCPv6 message size.** Maximum size of any DHCPv6 message the sender will be able to digest.
- **Class identifier.** Network managers can use this to specify that a client belongs to a given class that may need special or particular parameters.
- **Reconfigure multicast address.** The client may be required to join the supplied multicast address so as to receive reconfigure requests (see Section 10.2.6).
- **Renumber DHCPv6 server address.** If the DHCPv6 server has had its IP address changed, this extension will inform the clients of it.
- **Client-server authentication and client key selection.** These extensions provide end-to-end authentication of the client and server.

A way to create new extensions is also defined.

10.2.4 DHCP Reply

The server responds to the client's DHCP Request message with a DHCP reply, indicating in a status field the success or failure of the request. (Thus, DHCPACK and DHCPNAK are subsumed into one message type, with a richer set of replies than "Yes/No".)

The server will process the DHCP Request message and return an appropriate DHCP reply with extensions containing the requested parameters, or indicate a status code indicating why it couldn't.

10.2.5 DCHP Release

The client can release all or part of the resources allocated to it (IP addresses and so on) by sending a DHCP Release message to the appropriate server. Extensions can be used to indicate which resources are being released.

10.2.6 DHCP Reconfigure

Another new feature in DHCPv6 is the DHCP Reconfigure message. This message can be sent to a client to force it to start a new DHCP Request/DHCP Reply cycle. This provides a way for a network manager to peremptorily cause machines to reconfigure instead of having to work around the DHCPv4 lack of this feature. Workarounds like manually rebooting all affected machines or setting the default lease time very low a few days in advance all have drawbacks (there's always a machine locked in a room you don't have a key for, or the network traffic increases dramatically). Being able to send a DHCP Reconfigure is an answer to some network managers' prayers. Its inclusion in DHCPv6 is a direct result of its perceived lack in DHCPv4.

The client must listen continually on the DHCPv6 Port (546) for Reconfigure messages, and upon receipt, must send a DHCP Request to the server that

sent the Reconfigure. The DHCP Reconfigure message will contain extensions
indicating the parameters that must be reconfigured.

If the server had asked its clients to join a multicast Reconfigure group,
then it could reconfigure all of them at once by sending the DHCP Reconfigure
message to the group. The clients receiving this multicast Reconfigure message
must randomize their response times to avoid dumping a large load on the server
all at once.

10.3 Summary

IPv6 has been developed by the IETF in response to a need for continued Internet growth, and to incorporate new technology. DHCPv6 is a part of that effort,
and while it is still in development, bodes well to be a cleaner, more versatile
protocol than DHCPv4.

CHAPTER 11

The Future of DHCP

New Options for DHCP
Current Option Drafts
Secure DHCP
Reliable DHCP
How To Make a Difference

Predicting the future is always a risky business. Reading science fiction from as little as 20 years ago, one is struck with how *wrong* authors were about what things would be like at the turn of the millennium; both overly optimistic (we still have no practical flying cars) and overly pessimistic (we haven't blown the planet to bits yet).

Rather than take such a risk, I'm going to merely report on things that are in progress today, and speculate on what they mean for the near future. I'll still probably be wrong, but I'm less likely to be *very* wrong.

Of course, work on DHCP for IPv6 will continue to bring the protocol toward maturity, but that's all covered in the previous chapter.

11.1 New Options for DHCP

It's safe to say that new options will be defined for DHCP; there are more defined each year, for real or perceived needs of new networking hardware or software. This could be a problem; the IETF working group is starting to realize that it is very possible to run out of space for new option numbers. There are only 128 general options available after all, as the option codes from 128 to 255 are reserved for "site-specific" options.

One approach is to "recycle" dead options—ones that never made it out of the Internet Draft stage. Some Drafts get abandoned as people realize that maybe they don't need an option after all, or nobody cares enough to make it a standard. The option code is still assigned by IANA, though, and while it's possible to recycle some, it means tracking down the Draft's authors and making sure the number can be released.

Perhaps some site-specific numbers could be used as "regular" options. This could be a problem with sites that are already using their own options. To implement this properly would mean canvassing vendors and users for what site-specific option-codes they were using and coming up with a scheme for reserving some for "real" options. Again, this represents a lot of work, which will only delay the day when the option space is filled.

Another promising delay tactic is to postpone the assignment of an option code until it is moved out of Draft status. In other words, don't assign an actual code number until it becomes an RFC as a "proposed standard". This means that preliminary implementations would have to use the site-specific codes for initial experiments, but would alleviate the "dead option" problem.

Finally, a proposal to use one option number to lead to a "super option" is in Internet Draft stage. If this scheme were to be adopted, Option 127 would consist of a one-byte length and a two-byte "extended option" code. New options would be assigned extended codes, and 65,535 of them could be assigned before this space was filled. Other than the extended option code, the "super options" would work just like current options, only there could be more of them.

11.2 Current Option Drafts

Active Internet Drafts as of this writing (as always works in progress which may or may not go anywhere) include:

- **Option 127 extension.** This provides a mechanism for extending the option numbers once the eight-bits allocated (0 to 255) are used up.
- **Fully-qualified Domain Name Option.** This option allows the use of names rather than IP addresses in DHCP options, allowing the network manager to enter a list of names instead of a list of numbers.
- **User Class Option.** This option allows a client to specify a class it or its user belongs to (some servers already implement this).
- **POSIX Timezone Option.** Allows specification of the time zone of a client using strings defined in the POSIX standards.
- **Service Location Protocol Option.** Allows clients to locate directory agents when using the Service Location Protocol.
- **DHCP Agent Options.** Allows a relay agent to append information to DHCP messages sent between client and server; useful for cable modems and similar devices providing provisioning information.
- **Server Identification Option.** Allows servers to identify themselves in a DHCPOFFER with something other than their IP address.

- **Server Selection Option.** Allows servers to specify a value indicating their priority; clients can use it to choose between several servers. Similar to DHCPv6 server preference.

- **Proxy Client Configuration Option.** Allows servers to supply a list of URLs containing proxy configuration information; useful for things like Web browsers that must use a proxy server to get through a firewall.

- **Named Address Pool Option.** Allows a client to request that its address be assigned from a named pool of IP addresses.

- **Options for Locating LDAP Servers.** Allows servers to supply information about the location of local LDAP servers.

- **Domain Search List.** Allows the configuration of the list of domains used to resolve host names.

- **Continuation Option.** Allows options to be continued past the 256-octet limit imposed by the one-byte length field.

- **Subnet Selection.** Allows a client to choose which subnet its address should be assigned from. (Dial-up clients may all connect to a single physical server, yet wish to belong to different subnets, for example).

- **Multicast Extensions.** Extensions to DHCP to allow configuration of multicast clients.

- **Multicast Options.** Options to carry the information related to multicast configuration (see above).

- **Autonomous System Option and Server Range Option.** DHCP was explicitly not designed to configure routers (or "IP forwarders"); this option adds information needed by routing protocols.

Now, some of these Internet Drafts will become full standards and some will languish and expire. See the last section for information on helping to decide their outcome.

11.3 Secure DHCP

Why are people concerned about DHCP security? There are several possible problems.

First, unauthorized clients could gain access to a network by getting configuration information and a valid IP address from a DHCP server. This is not at all a far-fetched, paranoid fantasy. Many companies allow outsiders with laptop computers into conference rooms, and many of these conference rooms have network jacks. Plug in, reboot, and you're on the company internal network. Folks engaging in industrial espionage love this.

The flip side of unauthorized clients is, of course, unauthorized servers. Someone could set up a rogue server on a network and wreak havoc with client configurations. Either a simple denial of service could prevent clients from booting, or a clever saboteur could configure machines to route their packets through the rogue host, sniffing their contents and learning passwords or company secrets.

Second, a deliberate malicious attack could compromise both servers and clients. Servers could have their address pools exhausted and be unable to allocate addresses to legitimate clients. Clients could be configured with improper parameters.

To prevent these, and other unappealing scenarios from playing out, some kind of secure DHCP is necessary. The server needs to authenticate the client to ensure that the client is authorized to connect. At the same time, the client needs to authenticate the server to make sure this is a *real* server and not a fake. In addition, the server needs to authenticate relay agents, and the relay agents need to authenticate the server.

A popular method for authentication is public key cryptography (PKC), which is based on the difficulty of factoring very large numbers. An entity wishing to use PKC would create a pair of keys; one is the private key that must be kept secret, and the other the public key that can be given away freely. PKC is so designed that what is encrypted with one key can be decrypted only with the other. So, when a DHCP client wishes to prove to the server that its identity is correct, it can encrypt a token with the secret key that it alone knows and send it to the server. The server can use the client's public key to decrypt it, and if it gets the proper token, it can assume the message came from the client.

Data security can be addressed in a similar way, by either generating a cryptographic hash of the message or encrypting the hash. If the recipient generates the same hash, matching that obtained by decrypting the client's version, the recipient can assume the data was not altered between the sender and receiver.

Integrating these techniques into DHCP, and especially dealing with the problem of distributing the cryptographic keys is a "hot topic" in the DHCP working group. One major issue is that of key control and distribution. Whether DHCP transactions are authenticated with PKC or some other shared secret protocol, the private keys must somehow be transferred to the client machines, and must be protected so that they stay secret. Avoiding what some working group members call the "loading dock" problem is desired. In this problem, 1000 computers have just been delivered to the loading dock of your company, and your task is to get them all set up by tomorrow. Aside from the physical labor of moving and unpacking all those machines, clearly the less work you have to do to get them running the better. Ideally, they get plugged in, you fire up the DHCP client software, and get configured automatically. Fitting authenticated DHCP into this situation is more work. Solutions are not readily apparent, but are being assiduously sought.

11.4 Reliable DHCP

The DHCP standard allows more than one DHCP server to exist on a network, but provides no way for them to communicate with each other, or take over if the other fails. A current effort in the working group is attempting to address this problem, but the proposals are currently in a state of flux.

An early scheme was based on the Server Cache Synchronization Protocol used by ATM ARP servers to provide much of the same fail-safe functionality, but was seen as excessively complex by many of the participants. Lately a scheme called the "fail-over" protocol has been gaining acceptance. The current Draft provides for a pair-wise assignment of "primary" and "secondary" servers, with the secondary taking over when it detects that the primary has failed. The major goals of the proposal are that there be no interruption in service, that no address is ever assigned twice, and that when the primary is restored, service can easily revert to normal.

In normal operations, only the primary provides DHCP service; the secondary is idle. One could configure a server to be primary for one subnet, and secondary for another, and vice versa, of course.

There are three facets to the protocol. First, the primary sends periodic messages to keep the secondary informed of the contents of the lease database. Each time a binding is changed, a binding update message conveys this to the secondary. This way, they both have a current view of the world; a necessity for the secondary to take over properly.

Second, the secondary can identify the "upness" of the primary, so that it can decide when to take over. It does this by sending periodic poll messages to which the primary replies. If the reply does not arrive within a reasonable time, the secondary will assume the primary is down and take over. It will, of course, keep track of what it does while in command, and continue to poll to see if the primary is back.

Finally, when the primary comes back, the secondary has to coordinate an "orderly transfer of power" back to it. It stops DHCP service and sends binding update messages back to the primary, telling it what it did while the primary was out of service.

This protocol is being rapidly developed, and much more detail would be inappropriate; if you want more, consult the current Internet Draft.

11.5 How To Make a Difference

To participate in steering the future of DHCP, or any other Internet protocol, it's easy. Just join the appropriate IETF mailing lists and participate.

The IETF is not a membership-based organization; anyone who chooses to follow the mailing lists, attend meetings, and do work for the group is welcome.

The group charged with developing DHCP is the Dynamic Host Configuration working group. There are several mailing lists associated with it, all hosted at Bucknell University in Lewisburg, Pennsylvania. They are:

- General DHCP discussion: dhcp-v4@bucknell.edu
- Interaction between DHCP and DNS: dhcp-dns@bucknell.edu
- Implementation issues: dhcp-impl@bucknell.edu

- Bakeoff events: dhcp-bake@bucknell.edu
- Inter-server protocol: dhcp-serve@bucknell.edu
- DHCP for IPv6: dhcp-v6@bucknell.edu
- Implementation issues for DHCPv6: dhcp-v6impl@bucknell.edu

To subscribe to any of these mailing lists, send an email message to list-serv@bucknell.edu with the following line in the body of the message:

```
subscribe listname yourname
```

Be sure to change "listname" to the name of the list you want, and change "yourname" to, well, your name. For example, I subscribed to the dhcp-v4 list with this message:

```
To: listserv@bucknell.edu
From: berry@kerch.com (Berry Kercheval)

subscribe dhcp-v4 Berry Kercheval
```

A complete list of commands supported by Bucknell's mailing list processor will come back if you send it a message with HELP as the text.

Once you're subscribed, I recommend reading the messages for a few weeks before speaking up; make sure you understand what's going on. (This is good advice for joining *any* Internet group; lurk a while before posting.)

Good luck, and see you on the 'net!

Appendix A: DHCP Vendors

A number of organizations provide DHCP software, both client and server. Some do it as a commercial operation, some as a "public service", and some bundle it with other software (refer to Table A-1).

As a bit of a disclaimer, I feel I should mention that I work for Join Systems. Naturally I think you should all buy their product, but I'll cheerfully admit that other companies have decent products too. I'll try to be fair, despite my biases.

A-1 Summary of Available DHCP Implementations

Free			Commercial		
UNIX	**Windows**	**Macintosh**	**UNIX**	**Windows**	**Macintosh**
ISC	NT Server	–	JOIN	JOIN	Sonic Systems
CMU			AIC	Tellurian	Vicom
			MetaInfo	MetaInfo	
			TGV	Weird Solutions	

A.1 "Free" DHCP Servers

A.1.1 The Internet Software Consortium

Possibly the first place to go for DHCP software would be the Internet Software Consortium (ISC). ISC is a nonprofit corporation that sponsors development and maintenance of freely-distributable software.

Their software packages are:

- The Berkeley Internet Name Domain (BIND), which implements DNS.
- InterNetNews (INN), a widely used Usenet News server package.
- DHCP, an implementation of DHCP.

Their goal is to provide high-quality implementations of some of the Internet's core protocols, so that interoperability and the continued functioning of the Internet will be enhanced.

The ISC DHCP package includes a server, a client, and a relay agent.

Features include:

- Testing of IP addresses before assignment.
- Client exclusion.

Features planned for future releases are:

- Dynamic DNS support.
- DHCP authentication.
- DHCP database querys.
- Server-to-server protocol specification and implementation.

One very good reason for trying the ISC DHCP package is that it's free! It costs nothing but your time to download it from the ISC Web site and set it up. If it meets your needs, that's great. Many small-to-medium organizations have run happily for years with it.

Another reason is that source code to the package comes with it. If you need to change something or fix a bug, it's possible. The network of ISC users can help with support, or ISC itself offers a more formal support package for a fee.

You can find out more about the ISC DHCP package at:

```
http://ww.isc.org/dhcp.html
```

A.1.2 The CMU DHCP Server

Carnegie Mellon University uses their own simple DHCP server for their campus network, and makes it available for FTP. Find it at:

```
ftp://ftp.net.cmu.edu/pub/dhcp/
```

A.1.3 The Windows NT DHCP Server

Windows NT Server includes a DHCP server. It isn't really "free" because you have to pay for Windows NT Server to get it, but it doesn't cost *extra*.

The NT DHCP Server calls IP address ranges "scopes". All addresses in a scope must be on the same subnet.

There are three levels of DHCP options available. Global options apply to all scopes, but options can also be assigned on a scope-by-scope basis (also called "scope-specific" options). Finally, setting default options causes newly-created scopes to get those values.

The DHCP server keeps its databases in `%SystemRoot%\System32\dhcp`, and makes "backup copies" about once an hour. The location and frequency of backups can be changed with Registry entries.

Another Registry entry can force the server to rebuild the database from the backup on the next reboot.

Finally, yet another Registry entry controls the length of time an expired lease records remains in the database.

Find out more at:

```
http://www.microsoft.com/NTServer
```

A.2   Commercial DHCP Servers

This section contains some brief overviews of DHCP vendors; this list should not in any way be considered complete. Neither inclusion nor omission of a company or their product is intended to reflect on the quality of the product; this list is merely intended to give an idea of the scope of DHCP "solutions" available. If you are seriously looking for commercial, supported DHCP, you can use this list as a start, but do your homework before writing a purchase order, please.

A.2.1 Join Systems

A good example of a commercial DHCP product is JOIN, produced by Join Systems, Inc. Platforms supported are Sun Solaris 4.1 and 2.x, Solaris x86, HP-UX 10, Digital UNIX 4, and Windows NT 4.0. It has a broad and flexible range of administration and configuration options. Administration is by a Web-based interface (or an X-Motif helper application on UNIX platforms), but command line interfaces to all functions are available so that network managers can script their favorite operations.

Find out more at:

```
http://www.join.com
```

A.2.2 American Internet

American Internet's Network Registrar product provides Dynamic DNS and DHCP services. Address and name assignments are "published" with an LDAP interface. Supported platforms are Sun Sparc with Solaris 2 and NT 3.51 and 4.0.

Find out more at:

```
http://www.american.com/
```

A.2.3 MetaInfo

MetaInfo's product Meta IP includes Dynamic DNS, DHCP, and Remote Authentication Dial-In User Service (RADIUS) as well.

Meta IP's DHCP server supports fail-over to a secondary server for redundancy.

The suite of programs can be controlled with a centralized management system based on Java, and also support LDAP and SNMP.

Find out more at:

```
http://www.metainfo.com/
```

A.2.4 Cisco

Some Cisco routers provide DHCP server and relay agents.

Find out more at:

```
http://www.cisco.com
```

A.2.5 Tellurian

Tellurian's BootpdNT runs on Window NT (3.51 and 4.0), as well as Windows 95. A limited shareware version is available for test.

Find out more at:

```
http://www.tellurian.com.au/bootpdNT/
```

A.2.6 Vicom

Vicom Technologies supply a DHCP product that runs on MacOS with Open Transport. It is configured with a Graphical User Interface that conforms to Apple guidelines.

Find out more at:

```
http://www.vicomtech.com/dhcp/dhcp.main.html
```

Appendix B: DHCP Options

This appendix, specifically Table B-1, is a current list of DHCP options. Consult the RFC repositories for the latest information, of course. The options are grouped into logical groups, but the option codes were not all assigned at the same time or in order.

B-1 Variable-length Option Fields for DHCP Messages

TAG	LEN	NAME	DESCRIPTION
3	4N	Gateway	N IP addresses of routers for this subnet, in order of preference
4	4N	Time Server	N IP addresses of RFC-868 Time Servers
5	4N	IEN-116 Name Server	N IP addresses of Name Servers
6	4N	Domain Name Server	N IP addresses of DNS Servers
7	4N	Log Server	N IP addresses of Log Servers
8	4N	Cookie/Quote Server	N IP addresses of Quote-of-the-Day Servers
9	4N	LPR Server	N IP addresses of Printer Servers
10	4N	Impress Server	N IP addresses of Impress Servers

B-1 Variable-length Option Fields for DHCP Messages (Continued)

TAG	LEN	NAME	DESCRIPTION
11	4N	RLP Server	N IP addresses of Resource Location Servers
12	N	Hostname	Name of client
13	2	Boot File Size	Size of boot file in 512-byte blocks (unsigned 16-bit integer)
14	N	Merit Dump File	Pathname of file for a core dump
15	N	Domain Name	DNS name for this client
16	4	Swap Server	IP address of swap server
17	N	Root Path	Pathname to client's root disk
18	N	Extensions Path	Pathname of file with more extensions in it
Per-host IP Parameters			
19	1	IP Forwarding	If 1, enable IP forwarding; if 0 disable it
20	1	Non-local Source Routing	
21	8N	Policy Filter	Policy filters for non-local source routing
22	2	Maximum Datagram Reassembly	16-bit unsigned integer, maximum size datagram client will need to reassemble
23	1	Default IP TTL	Default TTL for transmitted packets
24	4	Path-MTU Aging Timeout	Time interval to use in path-MTH aging
25	2N	Path-MTU Plateau Table	List of MTU values to use in path-MTU discovery
Per-interface IP Parameters			
26	2	Interface MTU	MTU to use for a particular interface
27	1	All Subnets are Local	1 means client can assume all subnets of the network it is attached to should use the same MTU
28	4	Broadcast Address	IP Address to use for local broadcasts
29	1	Do Subnet Mask Discovery	1 means use ICMP to discover subnet mask
30	1	Mask Supplier	1 means respond to ICMP requests for subnet masks

B-1 Variable-length Option Fields for DHCP Messages (Continued)

TAG	LEN	NAME	DESCRIPTION
31	1	Do Router Discovery	1 means do RFC1256 router discovery
32	4	Router Solicitation Address	IP address to which client should send router solicitations
33	8N	Static Route	List of N static routes client should insert into routing table; list of IP address pairs: destination and corresponding router

Per-interface Link-layer Parameters

TAG	LEN	NAME	DESCRIPTION
34	1	Trailer Encapsulation	1 means use RFC893 trailer negotiation for ARP
35	4	ARP Cache Timeout	Time for ARP entries to live
36	1	Ethernet Encapsulation	1 means IEEE802.3 encapsulation, 0 means Ethernet V.2

TCP Parameters

TAG	LEN	NAME	DESCRIPTION
37	1	TCP Default TTL	Default time-to-live for TCP segments
38	4	TCP Keepalive	Seconds to wait before sending TCP keepalive
39	1	TCP Keepalive Garbage	1 means send an extra "garbage" byte for older TCP implementations

Application Parameters

TAG	LEN	NAME	DESCRIPTION
40	N	NIS Domain	NIS domain (not the same as DNS domain or Windows domain)
41	4N	NIS Servers	N IP addresses of NIS Servers
42	4N	NTP Servers	N IP addresses of Network Time Protocol Servers
43	N	Vendor-specific Info	Field-encoded according to vendor-specific extensions
44	4N	NetBIOS Name Server	N IP addresses of NetBIOS Name Servers
45	4N	NetBIOS Datagram Dist. Server	N IP addresses of NetBIOS Datagram Distribution Servers
46	1	NetBIOS Node Type	NetBios node type: 1 means B-node, 2 means P-node, 4 means M-node, 8 means H-node
47	N	NetBIOS Scope	NetBIOS over TCP/IP scope parameter

B-1 Variable-length Option Fields for DHCP Messages (Continued)

TAG	LEN	NAME	DESCRIPTION
48	4N	X Font Servers	N IP addresses of X Window System Font Server
49	4N	X Display Manager	N IP addresses of X Window System Display Managers

DHCP Options

TAG	LEN	NAME	DESCRIPTION
50	4	Requested IP Address	IP address requested by the client
51	4	IP Address Lease Time	Client can request lease time or server can set lease time using this option
52	1	Option Overload	1: file field holds options, 2: sname field holds options, 3: both hold options
53	1	DHCP Message Type	Type of DHCP message
54	4	DHCP Server Identifier	
55	N	Parameter Request	List of N option codes that the client wishes to get values for
56	N	Message	A string sent by a server, usually explaining an error for display to a human
57	2	Max DHCP Message Size	Largest DHCP message client will accept
58	4	Renewal (T1) Time	Time in seconds until client enters RENEWING state
59	4	Rebinding (T2) Time	Time in seconds until client enters REBINDING state
60	N	Vendor Class Identifier	String representing "class" of client; may be set by vendors in their client implementation; may contain configuration information
61	N	Client Identifier	"Opaque" identifier of the client; must be unique on client's subnet
64	N	NIS+ Domain	Name of NIS+ domain
65	4N	NIS+ Servers	N IP addresses of NIS+ Servers
66	N	TFTP Server Name	Name of TFTP server, if sname field has been used for option
67	N	Bootfile Name	Bootfile name, if file field has been used for options

B-1 Variable-length Option Fields for DHCP Messages (Continued)

TAG	LEN	NAME	DESCRIPTION
68	4N	Mobile IP Home Agent	N IP addresses of Mobile IP Home Agents
69	4N	SMTP Servers	N IP addresses of Simple Mail Transport Protocol Servers
70	4N	POP3 Servers	N IP addresses of Post Office Protocol V3 Servers
71	4N	NNTP Servers	N IP addresses of Network News Transport Protocol Servers
72	4N	WWW Servers	N IP addresses of WWW Servers
73	4N	Finger Servers	N IP addresses of Finger Servers
74	4N	IRC Servers	N IP addresses of Internet Relay Chat Servers
75	4N	StreetTalk Server	N IP addresses of StreetTalk Server
76	4N	StreetTalk DA Servers	N IP addresses of StreetTalk Directory Assistance Servers

Appendix C:
The Requests for Comments

This section contains the Requests for Comments, the standards-setting documents produced by the IETF. They are presented here for easy reference.

Only minimal reformatting has been done; the text of the documents is unaltered. Page numbering is, of course, redone.

The documents contained in this Appendix are shown in Table C-1 below.

C-1 RFCs Included in this Appendix

RFC Number	Title
951	· BOOTSTRAP PROTOCOL (BOOTP)
1048	BOOTP Vendor Information Extensions
2131	Dynamic Host Configuration Protocol
2132	DHCP Options and BOOTP Vendor Extensions

Network Working Group   Bill Croft (Stanford University)
Request for Comments: 951   John Gilmore (Sun Microsystems)
                                                    September 1985

BOOTSTRAP PROTOCOL (BOOTP)

1. Status of this Memo

This R FC suggests a proposed protocol for the ARPA-Internet community, and requests discussion and suggestions for improvements. Distribution of this memo is unlimited.

2. Overview

This RFC describes an IP/UDP bootstrap protocol (BOOTP) which allows a diskless client machine to discover its own IP address, the address of a server host, and the name of a file to be loaded into memory and executed. The bootstrap operation can be thought of as consisting of TWO PHASES. This RFC describes the first phase, which could be labeled 'address determination and bootfile selection'. After this address and filename information is obtained, control passes to the second phase of the bootstrap where a file transfer occurs. The file transfer will typically use the TFTP protocol [9], since it is intended that both phases reside in PROM on the client. However BOOTP could also work with other protocols such as SFTP [3] or FTP [6].

We suggest that the client's PROM software provide a way to do a complete bootstrap without 'user' interaction. This is the type of boot that would occur during an unattended power-up. A mechanism should be provided for the user to manually supply the necessary address and filename information to bypass the BOOTP protocol and enter the file transfer phase directly. If non-volatile storage is available, we suggest keeping default settings there and bypassing the BOOTP protocol unless these settings cause the file transfer phase to fail. If the cached information fails, the bootstrap should fall back to phase 1 and use BOOTP.

Here is a brief outline of the protocol:

1. A single packet exchange is performed. Timeouts are used to retransmit until a reply is received. The same packet field layout is used in both directions. Fixed length fields of maximum reasonable length are used to simplify structure definition and parsing.

2. An 'opcode' field exists with two values. The client broadcasts a 'bootrequest' packet. The server then answers with a 'bootreply' packet. The bootrequest contains the client's hardware address and its IP address, if known.

3. The request can optionally contain the name of the server the client wishes to respond. This is so the client can force the boot to occur from a specific host (e.g. if multiple versions of the same bootfile exist or if the server is in a far distant net/domain). The client does not have to deal with name / domain services; instead this function is pushed off to the BOOTP server.

4. The request can optionally contain the 'generic' filename to be booted. For example 'unix' or 'ethertip'. When the server sends the bootreply, it replaces this field with the fully qualified path name of the appropriate boot file. In determining this name, the server may consult his own database correlating the client's address and filename request, with a particular boot file customized for that client. If the bootrequest filename is a null string, then the server returns a filename field indicating the 'default' file to be loaded for that client.

5. In the case of clients who do not know their IP addresses, the server must also have a database relating hardware address to IP address. This client IP address is then placed into a field in the bootreply.

6. Certain network topologies (such as Stanford's) may be such that a given physical cable does not have a TFTP server directly attached to it (e.g. all the gateways and hosts on a certain cable may be diskless). With the cooperation of neighboring gateways, BOOTP can allow clients to boot off of servers several hops away, through these gateways. See the section 'Booting Through Gateways' below. This part of the protocol requires no special action on the part of the client. Implementation is optional and requires a small amount of additional code in gateways and servers.

3. Packet Format

All numbers shown are decimal, unless indicated otherwise. The BOOTP packet is enclosed in a standard IP [8] UDP [7] datagram. For simplicity it is assumed that the BOOTP packet is never fragmented. Any numeric fields shown are packed in 'standard network byte order', i.e. high order bits are sent first.

In the IP header of a bootrequest, the client fills in its own IP source address if known, otherwise zero. When the server address is unknown, the IP destination address will be the 'broadcast address' 255.255.255.255. This address means 'broadcast on the local cable, (I don't know my net number)' [4].

The UDP header contains source and destination port numbers. The BOOTP protocol uses two reserved port numbers, 'BOOTP client' (68) and 'BOOTP server' (67). The client sends requests using 'BOOTP server' as the destination port; this is usually a broadcast. The server sends replies using 'BOOTP client' as the destination port; depending on the kernel or driver facilities in the server, this may or may not be a broadcast (this is explained further in the section titled 'Chicken/Egg issues' below). The reason TWO reserved ports are used, is to avoid 'waking up' and scheduling the BOOTP server daemons, when a bootreply must be broadcast to a client. Since the server and other hosts won't be listening on the 'BOOTP client' port, any such incoming broadcasts will be filtered out at the kernel level. We could not simply allow the client to pick a 'random' port number for the UDP source port field; since the server reply may be broadcast, a randomly chosen port number could confuse other hosts that happened to be listening on that port.

The UDP length field is set to the length of the UDP plus BOOTP portions of the packet. The UDP checksum field can be set to zero by the client (or server) if desired, to avoid this extra overhead in a PROM implementation. In the 'Packet Processing' section below the phrase '[UDP checksum.]' is used whenever the checksum might be verified/computed.

FIELD	BYTES	DESCRIPTION
op	1	packet op code / message type. 1 = BOOTRE-QUEST, 2 = BOOTREPLY
htype	1	hardware address type, see ARP section in "Assigned Numbers" RFC. '1' = 10mb ethernet
hlen	1	hardware address length (eg '6' for 10mb ethernet).
hops	1	client sets to zero, optionally used by gateways in cross-gateway booting.
xid	4	transaction ID, a random number, used to match this boot request with the responses it generates.
secs	2	filled in by client, seconds elapsed since client started trying to boot.
--	2	unused
ciaddr	4	client IP address; filled in by client in bootrequest if known.
yiaddr	4	your' (client) IP address; filled by server if client doesn't know its own address (ciaddr was 0).
siaddr	4	server IP address; returned in bootreply by server.
giaddr	4	gateway IP address, used in optional cross-gateway booting.
chaddr	16	client hardware address, filled in by client.
sname	64	optional server host name, null terminated string.
file	128	boot file name, null terminated string; 'generic' name or null in bootrequest, fully qualified directory-path name in bootreply.
vend	64	optional vendor-specific area, e.g. could be hardware type/serial on request, or 'capability' / remote file system handle on reply. This info may be set aside for use by a third phase bootstrap or kernel.

4. Chicken / Egg Issues

How can the server send an IP datagram to the client, if the client doesnt know its own IP address (yet)? Whenever a bootreply is being sent, the transmitting machine performs the following operations:

1. If the client knows its own IP address ('ciaddr' field is nonzero), then the IP can be sent 'as normal', since the client will respond to ARPs [5].

2. If the client does not yet know its IP address (ciaddr zero), then the client cannot respond to ARPs sent by the transmitter of the bootreply. There are two options:

a. If the transmitter has the necessary kernel or driver hooKS to 'manually' construct an ARP address cache entry, then it can fill in an entry using the 'chaddr' and 'yiaddr' fields. Of course, this entry should have a timeout on it, just like any other entry made by the normal ARP code itself. The transmitter of the bootreply can then simply send the bootreply to the client's IP address. UNIX (4.2 BSD) has this capability.

b. If the transmitter lacks these kernel hooks, it can simply send the bootreply to the IP broadcast address on the appropriate interface. This is only one additional broadcast over the previous case.

5. Client Use of ARP

The client PROM must contain a simple implementation of ARP, e.g. the address cache could be just one entry in size. This will allow a second-phase-only boot (TFTP) to be performed when the client knows the IP addresses and bootfile name.

Any time the client is expecting to receive a TFTP or BOOTP reply, it should be prepared to answer an ARP request for its own IP to hardware address mapping (if known).

Since the bootreply will contain (in the hardware encapsulation) the hardware source address of the server/gateway, the client MAY be able to avoid sending an ARP request for the server/gateway IP address to be used in the following TFTP phase. However this should be treated only as a special case, since it is desirable to still allow a second-phase-only boot as described above.

6. Comparison to RARP

An earlier protocol, Reverse Address Resolution Protocol (RARP) [1] was proposed to allow a client to determine its IP address, given that it knew its hardware address. However RARP had the disadvantage that it was a hardware link level protocol (not IP/UDP based). This means that RARP could only be implemented on hosts containing special kernel or driver modifications to access these 'raw' packets. Since there are many network kernels existent now, with each source maintained by different organizations, a boot protocol that does not require kernel modifications is a decided advantage.

BOOTP provides this hardware to IP address lookup function, in addition to the other useful features described in the sections above.

7. Packet Processing

7.1. Client Transmission

Before setting up the packet for the first time, it is a good idea to clear the entire packet buffer to all zeros; this will place all fields in their default state. The client then creates a packet with the following fields.

The IP destination address is set to 255.255.255.255. (the broadcast address) or to the server's IP address (if known). The IP source address and 'ciaddr' are set to the client's IP address if known, else 0. The UDP header is set with the proper length; source port = 'BOOTP client' port destination port = 'BOOTP server' port.

'op' is set to '1', BOOTREQUEST. 'htype' is set to the hardware address type as assigned in the ARP section of the "Assigned Numbers" RFC. 'hlen' is set to the length of the hardware address, e.g. '6' for 10mb ethernet.

'xid' is set to a 'random' transaction id. 'secs' is set to the number of seconds that have elapsed since the client has started booting. This will let the servers know how long a client has been trying. As the number gets larger, certain servers may feel more 'sympathetic' towards a client they don't normally service. If a client lacks a suitable clock, it could construct a rough estimate using a loop timer. Or it could choose to simply send this field as always a fixed value, say 100 seconds.

If the client knows its IP address, 'ciaddr' (and the IP source address) are set to this value. 'chaddr' is filled in with the client's hardware address.

If the client wishes to restrict booting to a particular server name, it may place a null-terminated string in 'sname'. The name used should be any of the allowable names or nicknames of the desired host.

The client has several options for filling the 'file' name field. If left null, the meaning is 'I want to boot the default file for my machine'. A null file name can also mean 'I am only interested in finding out client/server/gateway IP addresses, I dont care about file names'.

The field can also be a 'generic' name such as 'unix' or 'gateway'; this means 'boot the named program configured for my machine'. Finally the field can be a fully directory qualified path name.

The 'vend' field can be filled in by the client with vendor-specific strings or structures. For example the machine hardware type or serial number may be placed here. However the operation of the BOOTP server should not DEPEND on this information existing.

If the 'vend' field is used, it is recommended that a 4 byte 'magic number' be the first item within 'vend'. This lets a server determine what kind of information it is seeing in this field. Numbers can be assigned by the usual 'magic number' process --you pick one and it's magic. A different magic number could be used for bootreply's than bootrequest's to allow the client to take special action with the reply information.

[UDP checksum.]

7.2. Client Retransmission Strategy

If no reply is received for a certain length of time, the client should retransmit the request. The time interval must be chosen carefully so as not to flood the network. Consider the case of a cable containing 100 machines that are just coming up after a power failure. Simply retransmitting the request every fou seconds will inundate the net.

As a possible strategy, you might consider backing off exponentially, similar to the way ethernet backs off on a collision. So for example if the first packet is at time 0:00, the second would be at :04, then :08, then :16, then :32, then :64. You should also randomize each time; this would be done similar to the ethernet specification by starting with a mask and 'and'ing that with with a random number to get the first backoff. On each succeeding backoff, the mask is increased in length by one bit. This doubles the average delay on each backoff.

After the 'average' backoff reaches about 60 seconds, it should be increased no further, but still randomized.

Before each retransmission, the client should update the 'secs' field. [UDP checksum.]

7.3. Server Receives BOOTREQUEST

[UDP checksum.] If the UDP destination port does not match the 'BOOTP server' port, discard the packet.

If the server name field (sname) is null (no particular server specified), or sname is specified and matches our name or nickname, then continue with packet processing.

If the sname field is specified, but does not match 'us', then there are several options:

1. You may choose to simply discard this packet.

2. If a name lookup on sname shows it to be on this same cable, discard the packet.

3. If sname is on a different net, you may choose to forward the packet to that address. If so, check the 'giaddr' (gateway address) field. If 'giaddr' is zero, fill it in with my address or the address of a gateway that can be used to get to that net. Then forward the packet.

If the client IP address (ciaddr) is zero, then the client does not know its own IP address. Attempt to lookup the client hardware address (chaddr, hlen, htype) in our database. If no match is found, discard the packet. Otherwise we now have an IP address for this client; fill it into the 'yiaddr' (your IP address) field.

We now check the boot file name field (file). The field will be null if the client is not interested in filenames, or wants the default bootfile. If the field is non-null, it is used as a lookup key in a database, along with the client's IP address. If there is a default file or generic file (possibly indexed by the client address) or a fully-specified path name that matches, then replace the 'file' field with the fully-specified path name of the selected boot file. If the field is non-null and no match was found, then the client is asking for a file we dont have; discard the packet, perhaps some other BOOTP server will have it.

The 'vend' vendor-specific data field should now be checked and if a recognized type of data is provided, client-specific actions should be taken, and a response placed in the 'vend' data field of he reply packet. For example, a workstation client could provide an authentication key and receive from the server a capability for remote file access, or a set of configuration options, which can be passed to the operating system that will shortly be booted in.

Place my (server) IP address in the 'siaddr' field. Set the 'op field to BOOTREPLY. The UDP destination port is set to 'BOOTP client'. If the client address 'ciaddr' is nonzero, send the packet there; else if the gateway address 'giaddr' is nonzero, set the UDP destination port to 'BOOTP server' and send the packet to 'giaddr'; else the client is on one of our cables but it doesnt know its own IP address yet --use a method described in the 'Egg' section above to send it to the client. If 'Egg' is used and we have multiple interfaces on this host, use the 'yiaddr' (your IP address) field to figure out which net (cable/interface) to send the packet to. [UDP checksum.]

7.4. Server/Gateway Receives BOOTREPLY

[UDP checksum.] If 'yiaddr' (your [the client's] IP address) refers to one of our cables, use one of the 'Egg' methods above to forward it to the client. Be sure to send it to the 'BOOTP client' UDP destination port.

7.5. Client Reception

Don't forget to process ARP requests for my own IP address (if I know it). [UDP checksum.] The client should discard incoming packets that: are not IP/ UDPs addressed to the boot port; are not BOOTREPLYs; do not match my IP address (if I know it) or my hardware address; do not match my transaction id. Otherwise we have received a successful reply. 'yiaddr' will contain my IP address, if I didnt know it before. 'file' is the name of the file name to TFTP 'read request'. The server address is in siaddr'. If 'giaddr' (gateway address) is nonzero, then the packets should be forwarded there first, in order to get to the server.

8. Booting Through Gateways

This part of the protocol is optional and requires some additional code in cooperating gateways and servers, but it allows cross-gateway booting. This is mainly useful when gateways are diskless machines. Gateways containing disks (e.g. a UNIX machine acting as a gateway), might as well run their own BOOTP/ TFTP servers.

Gateways listening to broadcast BOOTREQUESTs may decide to forward or rebroadcast these requests 'when appropriate'. For example, the gateway could have, as part of his configuration tables, a list of other networks or hosts to receive a copy of any broadcast BOOTREQUESTs. Even though a 'hops' field exists, it is a poor idea to simply globally rebroadcast the requests, since broadcast loops will almost certainly occur.

The forwarding could begin immediately, or wait until the 'secs' (seconds client has been trying) field passes a certain threshold.

If a gateway does decide to forward the request, it should look at the 'giaddr' (gateway IP address) field. If zero, it should plug its own IP address (on the receiving cable) into this field. It may also use the 'hops' field to optionally control how far the packet is reforwarded. Hops should be incremented on each forwarding. For example, if hops passes '3', the packet should probably be discarded. [UDP checksum.]

Here we have recommended placing this special forwarding function in the gateways. But that does not have to be the case. As long as some 'BOOTP forwarding agent' exists on the net with the booting client, the agent can do the forwarding when appropriate. Thus this service may or may not be co-located with the gateway.

In the case of a forwarding agent not located in the gateway, the agent could save himself some work by plugging the broadcast address of the interface receiving the bootrequest into the 'giaddr' field. Thus the reply would get forwarded using normal gateways, not involving the forwarding agent. Of course the disadvantage here is that you lose the ability to use the 'Egg' non-broadcast method of sending the reply, causing extra overhead for every host on the client cable.

9. Sample BOOTP Server Database

As a suggestion, we show a sample text file database that the BOOTP server program might use. The database has two sections, delimited by a line containing an percent in column 1. The first section contains a 'default directory' and mappings from generic names to directory/pathnames. The first generic name in this section is the 'default file' you get when the bootrequest contains a null 'file' string.

The second section maps hardware addresstype/address into an ipaddress. Optionally you can also overide the default generic name by supplying a ipaddress specific genericname. A 'suffix' item is also an option; if supplied, any generic names specified by the client will be accessed by first appending 'suffix' to the 'pathname' appropriate to that generic name. If that file is not found, then the plain 'pathname' will be tried. This 'suffix' option allows a whole set of custom generics to be setup without a lot of effort. Below is shown the general format; fields are delimited by one or more spaces or tabs; trailing empty fields may be omitted; blank lines and lines beginning with '#' are ignored.

```
# comment line
    homedirectory  genericname1 pathname1  genericname2
pathname2 ...
    % end of generic names, start of address mappings
    hostname1 hardwaretype hardwareaddr1 ipaddr1 genericname
suffix
hostname2 hardwaretype hardwareaddr2 ipaddr2 genericname
suffix  ...
```

Here is a specific example. Note the 'hardwaretype' number is the same as that shown in the ARP section of the 'Assigned Numbers' RFC. The 'hardwaretype' and 'ipaddr' numbers are in decimal; 'hardwareaddr' is in hex.

```
    # last updated by smith
    /usr/boot
    vmunix          vmunix
    tip             ethertip
    watch           /usr/diag/etherwatch
    gate            gate.
    % end of generic names, start of address mappings
    hamilton      1 02.60.8c.06.34.98   36.19.0.5
    burr          1 02.60.8c.34.11.78   36.44.0.12
    101-gateway   1 02.60.8c.23.ab.35   36.44.0.32    gate 101
    mjh-gateway   1 02.60.8c.12.32.bc   36.42.0.64    gate mjh
    welch-tipa    1 02.60.8c.22.65.32   36.47.0.14    tip
    welch-tipb    1 02.60.8c.12.15.c8   36.46.0.12    tip
```

In the example above, if 'mjh-gateway' does a default boot, it will get the file '/usr/boot/gate.mjh'.

10. Acknowledgements

Ross Finlayson (et. al.) produced two earlier RFC's discussing TFTP bootstraping [2] using RARP [1].

We would also like to acknowledge the previous work and comments of Noel Chiappa, Bob Lyon, Jeff Mogul, Mark Lewis, and David Plummer.

REFERENCES

1. Ross Finlayson, Timothy Mann, Jeffrey Mogul, Marvin Theimer. A Reverse Address Resolution

2. Ross Finlayson. Bootstrap Loading using TFTP. RFC 906, NIC, June, 1984.

3. Mark Lottor. Simple File Transfer Protocol. RFC 913, NIC, September, 1984.

4. Jeffrey Mogul. Broadcasting Internet Packets. RFC 919, NIC, October, 1984.

5. David Plummer. An Ethernet Address Resolution Protocol. RFC 826, NIC, September, 1982.

6. Jon Postel. File Transfer Protocol. RFC 765, NIC, June, 1980.

7. Jon Postel. User Datagram Protocol. RFC 768, NIC, August, 1980.

8. Jon Postel. Internet Protocol. RFC 791, NIC, September, 1981.

9. K. R. Sollins, Noel Chiappa. The TFTP Protocol. RFC 783, NIC, June, 1981.

Network Working Group   P. Prindeville
Request for Comments: 1048   McGill University
                                                             February 1988

BOOTP Vendor Information Extensions

Status of this Memo

This memo proposes an addition to the Bootstrap Protocol (BOOTP). Comments and suggestions for improvements are sought. Distribution of this memo is unlimited.

Introduction

As workstations and personal computers proliferate on the Internet, the administrative complexity of maintaining a network is increased by an order of magnitude. The assignment of local network resources to each client represents one such difficulty. In most environments, delegating such responsibility to the user is not plausible and, indeed, the solution is to define the resources in uniform terms, and to automate their assignment.

The basic Bootstrap Protocol [RFC-951] dealt with the issue of assigning an internet address to a client, as well as a few other resources. The protocol included provisions for vendor-defined resource information.

This memo defines a (potentially) vendor-independent interpretation of this resource information.

Overview of BOOTP

While the Reverse Address Resolution (RARP) Protocol [RFC-903] may be used to assign an IP address to a local network hardware address, it provides only part of the functionality needed. Though this protocol can be used in conjunction with other supplemental protocols (the Resource Location Protocol [RFC-887], the Domain Name System [RFC- 883]), a more integrated solution may be desirable.

Bootstrap Protocol (BOOTP) is a UDP/IP-based protocol that allows a booting host to configure itself dynamically, and more significantly, without user supervision. It provides a means to assign a host its IP address, a file from which to download a boot program from some server, that server's address, and (if present) the address of an Internet gateway.

One obvious advantage of this procedure is the centralized management of network addresses, which eliminates the need for per-host unique configuration files. In an environment with several hundred hosts, maintaining local configuration information and operating system versions specific to each host might otherwise become chaotic. By categorizing hosts into classes and maintaining configuration information and boot programs for each class, the complexity of this chore may be reduced in magnitude.

BOOTP Vendor Information Format

The full description of the BOOTP request/reply packet format may be found in [RFC-951]. The rest of this document will concern itself with the last field of the packet, a 64 octet area reserved for vendor information, to be used in a hitherto unspecified fashion. A generalized use of this area for giving information useful to a wide class of machines, operating systems, and configurations follows. In situations where a single BOOTP server is to be used among heterogeneous clients in a single site, a generic class of data may be used.

Vendor Information "Magic Cookie"

As suggested in [RFC-951], the first four bytes of this field have been assigned to the magic cookie, which identifies the mode in which the succeeding data is to be interpreted. The value of the magic cookie is the 4 octet dotted decimal 99.130.83.99 (or hexadecimal number 63.82.53.63) in network byte order.

Format of Individual Fields

The vendor information field has been implemented as a free format, with extendable tagged sub-fields. These sub-fields are length tagged (with exceptions; see below), allowing clients not implementing certain types to correctly skip fields they cannot interpret. Lengths are exclusive of the tag and length octets; all multi-byte quantities are in network byte-order.

Fixed Length Data

The fixed length data are comprised of two formats. Those that have no data consist of a single tag octet and are implicitly of one-octet length, while those that contain data consist of one tag octet, one length octet, and length octets of data.

Pad Field (Tag: 0, Data: None)

May be used to align subsequent fields to word boundaries required by the target machine (i.e., 32-bit quantities such as IP addresses on 32-bit boundaries).

Subnet Mask Field (Tag: 1, Data: 4 subnet mask bytes)

Specifies the net and local subnet mask as per the standard on subnetting [RFC-950]. For convenience, this field must precede the GATEWAY field (below), if present.

Time Offset Field (Tag: 2, Data: 4 time offset bytes)

Specifies the time offset of the local subnet in seconds from Coordinated Universal Time (UTC); signed 32-bit integer.

End Field (Tag: 255, Data: None)

Specifies end of usable data in the vendor information area. The rest of this field should be filled with PAD zero) octets.

Variable Length Data

The variable length data has a single format; it consists of one tag octet, one length octet, and length octets of data.

Gateway Field (Tag: 3, Data: N address bytes)

Specifies the IP addresses of N/4 gateways for this subnet. If one of many gateways is preferred, that should be first.

Time Server Field (Tag: 4, Data: N address bytes)

Specifies the IP addresses of N/4 time servers [RFC-868].

IEN-116 Name Server Field (Tag: 5, Data: N address bytes)

Specifies the IP addresses of N/4 name servers [IEN-116].

Domain Name Server Field (Tag: 6, Data: N address bytes)

Specifies the IP addresses of N/4 domain name servers RFC- 883].

Log Server Field (Tag: 7, Data: N address bytes)

Specifies the IP addresses of N/4 MIT-LCS UDP log server [LOGGING].

Cookie/Quote Server Field (Tag: 8, Data: N address bytes)

Specifies the IP addresses of N/4 Quote of the Day servers [RFC-865].

LPR Server Field (Tag: 9, Data: N address bytes)

Specifies the IP addresses of N/4 Berkeley 4BSD printer servers [LPD].

Impress Server Field (Tag: 10, Data: N address bytes)

Specifies the IP addresses of N/4 Impress network image servers [IMAGEN].

RLP Server Field (Tag: 11, Data: N address bytes)

Specifies the IP addresses of N/4 Resource Location Protocol (RLP) servers [RFC-887].

Hostname (Tag: 12, Data: N bytes of hostname)

Specifies the name of the client. The name may or may not domain qualified: this is a site-specific issue.

Reserved Fields (Tag: 128-254, Data: N bytes of undefined content)

Specifies additional site-specific information, to be interpreted on an implementation-specific basis. This should follow all data with the preceding generic tags 0- 127).

Extensions

Additional generic data fields may be registered by contacting:

Joyce K. Reynolds

USC - Information Sciences Institute

4676 Admiralty Way

Marina del Rey, California 90292-6695

or by E-mail as: JKREYNOLDS@ISI.EDU (nic handle JKR1).

Implementation specific use of undefined generic types (those in the range 12-127) may conflict with other implementations, and registration is required.

When selecting information to put into the vendor specific area, care should be taken to not exceed the 64 byte length restriction. Nonessential information (such as host name and quote of the day server) may be excluded, which may later be located with a more appropriate service protocol, such as RLP or the WKS resource-type of the domain name system. Indeed, even RLP servers may be discovered using a broadcast request to locate a local RLP server.

Comparison to Alternative Approaches

Extending BOOTP to provide more configuration information than the minimum required by boot PROMs may not be necessary. Rather than having each module in a host (e.g., the time module, the print spooler, the domain name resolver) broadcast to the BOOTP server to obtain the addresses of required servers, it would be better for each of them to multicast directly to the particular server group of interest, possibly using "expanding ring" multicasts.

The multicast approach has the following advantages over the BOOTP approach:

- It eliminates dependency on a third party (the BOOTP server) that may be temporarily unavailable or whose database may be incorrect or incomplete. Multicasting directly to the desired services will locate those servers that are currently available, and only those.
- It reduces the administrative chore of keeping the (probably replicated) BOOTP database up-to-date and consistent. This is especially important in an environment with a growing number of services and an evolving population of servers.
- In some cases, it reduces the amount of packet traffic and/or the delay required to get the desired information. For example, the current time can be obtained by a single multicast to a time server group which evokes replies from those time servers that are currently up. The BOOTP approach would require a broadcast to the BOOTP server, a reply from the BOOTP server, one or more unicasts to time servers (perhaps waiting for long timeouts if the initially chosen server(s) are down), and finally a reply from a server.

One apparent advantage of the proposed BOOTP extensions is that they provide a uniform way to locate servers. However, the multicast approach could also be implemented in a consistent way across multiple services. The V System naming protocol is a good example of this; character string pathnames are used to name any number of resources (i.e., not just files) and a standard subroutine library looks after multicasting to locate the resources, caching the discovered locations, and detecting stale cache data.

Another apparent advantage of the BOOTP approach is that it allows an administrator to easily control which hosts use which servers. The multicast approach favors more distributed control over resource allocation, where each server decides which hosts it will serve, using whatever level of authentication is appropriate for the particular service. For example, time servers usually don't care who they serve (i.e., administrative control via the BOOTP database is unnecessary), whereas file servers usually require strong authentication (i.e., administrative control via the BOOTP database is insufficient).

The main drawback of the multicast approach, of course, is that IP multicasting is not widely implemented, and there is a need to locate existing services which do not understand IP multicasts.

The BOOTP approach may be most efficient in the case that all the information needed by the client host is returned by a single BOOTP reply and each program module simply reads the information it needs from a local table filled in by the BOOTP reply.

Acknowledgments

I would like to thank the following persons for their helpful comments and insights into this memo: Drew Perkins, of Carnagie Mellon University, Bill Croft, of Stanford University, and co-author of BOOTP, and Steve Deering, also of Stanford University, for contributing the "Comparison to Alternative Approaches" section.

References

[RFC-951] Croft, B., and J. Gilmore, "Bootstrap Protocol", Network Information Center, SRI International, Menlo Park, California, September 1985.

[RFC-903] Finlayson, R., T. Mann, J. Mogul, and M. Theimer, "A Reverse Address Resolution Protocol", Network Information Center, SRI International, Menlo Park, California, June 1984.

[RFC-887] Accetta, M., "Resource Location Protocol", Network Information Center, SRI International, Menlo Park, California, December 1983.

[RFC-883] Mockapetris, P., "Domain Name - Implementation and Specification", Network Information Center, SRI International, Menlo Park, California, November 1983.

[RFC-950] Mogul, J., "Internet Standard Subnetting Procedure", Network Information Center, SRI International, Menlo Park, California, August 1985.

[RFC-868] Postel, J., "Time Protocol", Network Information Center, SRI International, Menlo Park, California, May 1983.

[IEN-116] Postel, J., "Internet Name Server", Network Information Center, SRI International, Menlo Park, California, August 1979.

[LOGGING] Clark, D., Logging and Status Protocol", Massachusetts Institute of Technology Laboratory for Computer Science, Cambridge, Massachusetts, 1981.

[RFC-865] Postel, J., "Quote of the Day Protocol", Network Information Center, SRI International, Menlo Park, California, May 1983.

[LPD] Campbell, R., "4.2BSD Line Printer Spooler Manual", UNIX Programmer's Manual, Vol II, University of California at Berkeley, Computer Science Division, July 1983.

[IMAGEN] "Image Server XT Programmer's Guide", Imagen Corporation, Santa Clara, California, August 1986.

Network Working Group   R. Droms
Request for Comments: 2131   Bucknell University
Obsoletes: 1541   March 1997
Category: Standards Track

Dynamic Host Configuration Protocol

Status of this memo

Abstract

The Dynamic Host Configuration Protocol (DHCP) provides a framework for passing configuration information to hosts on a TCPIP network. DHCP is based on the Bootstrap Protocol (BOOTP) [7], adding the capability of automatic allocation of reusable network addresses and additional configuration options [19]. DHCP captures the behavior of BOOTP relay agents [7, 21], and DHCP participants can interoperate with BOOTP participants [9].

Table of Contents

1. Introduction

The Dynamic Host Configuration Protocol (DHCP) provides configuration parameters to Internet hosts. DHCP consists of two components: a protocol for delivering host-specific configuration parameters from a DHCP server to a host and a mechanism for allocation of network addresses to hosts.

DHCP is built on a client-server model, where designated DHCP server hosts allocate network addresses and deliver configuration parameters to dynamically configured hosts. Throughout the remainder of this document, the term "server" refers to a host providing initialization parameters through DHCP, and the term "client" refers to a host requesting initialization parameters from a DHCP server.

A host should not act as a DHCP server unless explicitly configured to do so by a system administrator. The diversity of hardware and protocol implementations in the Internet would preclude reliable operation if random hosts were allowed to respond to DHCP requests. For example, IP requires the setting of many parameters within the protocol implementation software. Because IP can be used on many dissimilar kinds of network hardware, values for those parameters cannot be guessed or assumed to have correct defaults. Also, distributed address allocation schemes depend on a polling/defense mechanism for discovery of addresses that are already in use. IP hosts may not always be able to defend their network addresses, so that such a distributed address allocation scheme cannot be guaranteed to avoid allocation of duplicate network addresses.

DHCP supports three mechanisms for IP address allocation. In "automatic allocation", DHCP assigns a permanent IP address to a client. In "dynamic allocation", DHCP assigns an IP address to a client for a limited period of time (or until the client explicitly relinquishes the address). In "manual allocation", a client's IP address is assigned by the network administrator, and DHCP is used simply to convey the assigned address to the client. A particular network will use one or more of these mechanisms, depending on the policies of the network administrator.

Dynamic allocation is the only one of the three mechanisms that allows automatic reuse of an address that is no longer needed by the client to which it was assigned. Thus, dynamic allocation is particularly useful for assigning an address to a client that will be connected to the network only temporarily or for sharing a limited pool of IP addresses among a group of clients that do not need permanent IP addresses. Dynamic allocation may also be a good choice for assigning an IP address to a new client being permanently connected to a network where IP addresses are sufficiently scarce that it is important to reclaim them when old clients are retired. Manual allocation allows DHCP to be used to eliminate the error-prone process of manually configuring hosts with IP addresses in environments where (for whatever reasons) it is desirable to manage IP address assignment outside of the DHCP mechanisms.

The format of DHCP messages is based on the format of BOOTP messages, to capture the BOOTP relay agent behavior described as part of the BOOTP specification [7, 21] and to allow interoperability of existing BOOTP clients with DHCP servers. Using BOOTP relay agents eliminates the necessity of having a DHCP server on each physical network segment.

1.1 Changes to RFC 1541

This document updates the DHCP protocol specification that appears in RFC1541. A new DHCP message type, DHCPINFORM, has been added; see section 3.4, 4.3 and 4.4 for details. The classing mechanism for identifying DHCP clients to DHCP servers has been extended to include "vendor" classes as defined in sections 4.2 and 4.3. The minimum lease time restriction has been removed. Finally, many editorial changes have been made to clarify the text as a result of experience gained in DHCP interoperability tests.

1.2 Related Work

There are several Internet protocols and related mechanisms that address some parts of the dynamic host configuration problem. The Reverse Address Resolution Protocol (RARP) [10] (through the extensions defined in the Dynamic RARP (DRARP) [5]) explicitly addresses the problem of network address discovery, and includes an automatic IP address assignment mechanism. The Trivial File Transfer Protocol (TFTP) [20] provides for transport of a boot image from a boot server. The Internet Control Message Protocol (ICMP) [16] provides for informing hosts of additional routers via "ICMP redirect" messages. ICMP also can provide subnet mask information through the "ICMP mask request" message and other information through the (obsolete) "ICMP information request" message. Hosts can locate routers through the ICMP router discovery mechanism [8].

BOOTP is a transport mechanism for a collection of configuration information. BOOTP is also extensible, and official extensions [17] have been defined for several configuration parameters. Morgan has proposed extensions to BOOTP for dynamic IP address assignment [15]. The Network Information Protocol (NIP), used by the Athena project at MIT, is a distributed mechanism for dynamic IP address assignment [19]. The Resource Location Protocol RLP [1] provides for location of higher level services. Sun Microsystems diskless workstations use a boot procedure that employs RARP, TFTP and an RPC mechanism called "bootparams" to deliver configuration information and operating system code to diskless hosts. (Sun Microsystems, Sun Workstation and SunOS are trademarks of Sun Microsystems, Inc.) Some Sun networks also use DRARP and an auto-installation mechanism to automate the configuration of new hosts in an existing network.

In other related work, the path minimum transmission unit (MTU) discovery algorithm can determine the MTU of an arbitrary internet path [14]. The Address Resolution Protocol (ARP) has been proposed as a transport protocol for resource location and selection [6]. Finally, the Host Requirements RFCs [3, 4] mention specific requirements for host reconfiguration and suggest a scenario for initial configuration of diskless hosts.

1.3 Problem definition and issues

DHCP is designed to supply DHCP clients with the configuration parameters defined in the Host Requirements RFCs. After obtaining parameters via DHCP, a DHCP client should be able to exchange packets with any other host in the Internet. The TCP/IP stack parameters supplied by DHCP are listed in Appendix A.

Not all of these parameters are required for a newly initialized client. A client and server may negotiate for the transmission of only those parameters required by the client or specific to a particular subnet.

DHCP allows but does not require the configuration of client parameters not directly related to the IP protocol. DHCP also does not address registration of newly configured clients with the Domain Name System (DNS) [12, 13].

DHCP is not intended for use in configuring routers.

1.4 Requirements

Throughout this document, the words that are used to define the significance of particular requirements are capitalized. These words are:

"MUST". This word or the adjective "REQUIRED" means that the item is an absolute requirement of this specification.

"MUST NOT". This phrase means that the item is an absolute prohibition of this specification.

"SHOULD". This word or the adjective "RECOMMENDED" means that there may exist valid reasons in particular circumstances to ignore this item, but the full implications should be understood and the case carefully weighed before choosing a different course.

"SHOULD NOT". This phrase means that there may exist valid reasons in particular circumstances when the listed behavior is acceptable or even useful, but the full implications should be understood and the case carefully weighed before implementing any behavior described with this label.

"MAY". This word or the adjective "OPTIONAL" means that this item is truly optional. One vendor may choose to include the item because a particular marketplace requires it or because it enhances the product, for example; another vendor may omit the same item.

1.5 Terminology

This document uses the following terms:

"DHCP client". A DHCP client is an Internet host using DHCP to obtain configuration parameters such as a network address.

"DHCP server". A DHCP server is an Internet host that returns configuration parameters to DHCP clients.

"BOOTP relay agent". BOOTP relay agent or relay agent is an Internet host or router that passes DHCP messages between DHCP clients and DHCP servers.

DHCP is designed to use the same relay agent behavior as specified in the BOOTP protocol specification.

"binding". A binding is a collection of configuration parameters, including at least an IP address, associated with or "bound to" a DHCP client. Bindings are managed by DHCP servers.

1.6 Design goals

The following list gives general design goals for DHCP.

- DHCP should be a mechanism rather than a policy. DHCP must allow local system administrators control over configuration parameters where desired; e.g., local system administrators should be able to enforce local policies concerning allocation and access to local resources where desired.

- Clients should require no manual configuration. Each client should be able to discover appropriate local configuration parameters without user intervention and incorporate those parameters into its own configuration.

- Networks should require no manual configuration for individual clients. Under normal circumstances, the network manager should not have to enter any per-client configuration parameters.

- DHCP should not require a server on each subnet. To allow for scale and economy, DHCP must work across routers or through the intervention of BOOTP relay agents.
- A DHCP client must be prepared to receive multiple responses to a request for configuration parameters. Some installations may include multiple, overlapping DHCP servers to enhance reliability and increase performance.
- DHCP must coexist with statically configured, non-participating hosts and with existing network protocol implementations.
- DHCP must interoperate with the BOOTP relay agent behavior as described by RFC 951 and by RFC 1542 [21].
- DHCP must provide service to existing BOOTP clients.

The following list gives design goals specific to the transmission of the network layer parameters. DHCP must:

- Guarantee that any specific network address will not be in use by more than one DHCP client at a time,
- Retain DHCP client configuration across DHCP client reboot. A DHCP client should, whenever possible, be assigned the same configuration parameters (e.g., network address) in response to each request,
- Retain DHCP client configuration across server reboots, and, whenever possible, a DHCP client should be assigned the same configuration parameters despite restarts of the DHCP mechanism,
- Allow automated assignment of configuration parameters to new clients to avoid hand configuration for new clients,
- Support fixed or permanent allocation of configuration parameters to specific clients.

2. Protocol Summary

From the client's point of view, DHCP is an extension of the BOOTP mechanism. This behavior allows existing BOOTP clients to interoperate with DHCP servers without requiring any change to the clients' initialization software. RFC 1542 [2] details the interactions between BOOTP and DHCP clients and servers [9]. There are some new, optional transactions that optimize the interaction between DHCP clients and servers that are described in sections 3 and 4.

Figure 1 gives the format of a DHCP message and table 1 describes each of the fields in the DHCP message. The numbers in parentheses indicate the size of each field in octets. The names for the fields given in the figure will be used throughout this document to refer to the fields in DHCP messages.

There are two primary differences between DHCP and BOOTP. First, DHCP defines mechanisms through which clients can be assigned a network address for a finite lease, allowing for serial reassignment of network addresses to different clients. Second, DHCP provides the mechanism for a client to acquire all of the IP configuration parameters that it needs in order to operate.

DHCP introduces a small change in terminology intended to clarify the meaning of one of the fields. What was the "vendor extensions" field in BOOTP has been re-named the "options" field in DHCP. Similarly, the tagged data items that were used inside the BOOTP "vendor extensions" field, which were formerly referred to as "vendor extensions," are now termed simply "options."

```
 0                   1                   2                   3
 0 1 2 3 4 5 6 7 8 9 0 1 2 3 4 5 6 7 8 9 0 1 2 3 4 5 6 7 8 9 0 1
+-+-+-+-+-+-+-+-+-+-+-+-+-+-+-+-+-+-+-+-+-+-+-+-+-+-+-+-+-+-+-+-+
|     op (1)    |   htype (1)   |   hlen (1)    |   hops (1)    |
+---------------+---------------+---------------+---------------+
|                            xid (4)                            |
+-------------------------------+-------------------------------+
|           secs (2)            |           flags (2)           |
+-------------------------------+-------------------------------+
|                          ciaddr  (4)                          |
+---------------------------------------------------------------+
|                          yiaddr  (4)                          |
+---------------------------------------------------------------+
|                          siaddr  (4)                          |
+---------------------------------------------------------------+
|                          giaddr  (4)                          |
+---------------------------------------------------------------+
|                                                               |
|                          chaddr  (16)                         |
|                                                               |
|                                                               |
+---------------------------------------------------------------+
|                                                               |
|                          sname   (64)                         |
+---------------------------------------------------------------+
|                                                               |
|                          file    (128)                        |
+---------------------------------------------------------------+
|                                                               |
|                       options (variable)                      |
+---------------------------------------------------------------+
```

Figure 1: Format of a DHCP message

DHCP defines a new 'client identifier' option that is used to pass an explicit client identifier to a DHCP server. This change eliminates the overloading of the 'chaddr' field in BOOTP messages, where 'chaddr' is used both as a hardware address for transmission of BOOTP reply messages and as a client identifier. The 'client identifier' is an opaque key, not to be interpreted by the server; for example, the 'client identifier' may contain a hardware address, identical to the contents of the 'chaddr' field, or it may contain another type of identifier, such as a DNS name. The 'client identifier' chosen by a DHCP client MUST be unique to that client within the subnet to which the client is attached. If the client uses a 'client identifier' in one message, it MUST use that same identifier in all subsequent messages, to ensure that all servers correctly identify the client.

DHCP clarifies the interpretation of the 'siaddr' field as the address of the server to use in the next step of the client's bootstrap process. A DHCP server may return its own address in the 'siaddr' field, if the server is prepared to supply the next bootstrap service (e.g., delivery of an operating system executable image). A DHCP server always returns its own address in the 'server identifier' option.

```
FIELD       OCTETS   DESCRIPTION
-----       ------   -----------
op          1        Message op code / message type.
                     1 = BOOTREQUEST, 2 = BOOTREPLY
htype       1        Hardware address type, see ARP section in
                     "Assigned Numbers" RFC; e.g., '1' = 10mb
                     ethernet.
hlen        1        Hardware address length (e.g.  '6' for 10mb
                     ethernet).
hops        1        Client sets to zero, optionally used by
                     relay agents when booting via a relay agent.
xid         4        Transaction ID, a random number chosen by
                     the client, used by the client and server to
                     associate messages and responses between a
                     client and a server.
secs        2        Filled in by client, seconds elapsed since
                     client began address acquisition or renewal
                     process.
flags       2        Flags (see figure 2).
ciaddr      4        Client IP address; only filled in if client
                     is in BOUND, RENEW or REBINDING state and
                     can respond to ARP requests.
yiaddr      4        'your' (client) IP address.
siaddr      4        IP address of next server to use in boot-
                     strap; returned in DHCPOFFER, DHCPACK by
                     server.
giaddr      4        Relay agent IP address, used in booting via
                     a relay agent.
chaddr      16       Client hardware address.
sname       64       Optional server host name, null terminated
                     string.
file        128      Boot file name, null terminated string;
                     "generic" name or null in DHCPDISCOVER,
                     fully qualified directory-path name in
                     DHCPOFFER.
options     var      Optional parameters field.  See the options
                     documents for a list of defined options.
```

Table 1: Description of fields in a DHCP message

The 'options' field is now variable length. A DHCP client must be prepared to receive DHCP messages with an 'options' field of at least length 312 octets. This requirement implies that a DHCP client must be prepared to receive a message of up to 576 octets, the minimum IP datagram size an IP host must be prepared to accept [3]. DHCP clients may negotiate the use of larger DHCP messages through the 'maximum DHCP message size' option. The options field may be further extended into the 'file' and 'sname' fields.

In the case of a client using DHCP for initial configuration (before the client's TCP/IP software has been completely configured), DHCP requires creative use of the client's TCP/IP software and liberal interpretation of RFC 1122. The TCP/IP software SHOULD accept and forward to the IP layer any IP packets delivered to the client's hardware address before the IP address is configured; DHCP servers and BOOTP relay agents may not be able to deliver DHCP messages to clients that cannot accept hardware unicast datagrams before the TCP/IP software is configured.

To work around some clients that cannot accept IP unicast datagrams before the TCP/IP software is configured as discussed in the previous paragraph, DHCP uses the 'flags' field [21]. The leftmost bit is defined as the BROADCAST (B) flag. The semantics of this flag are discussed in section 4.1 of this document. The remaining bits of the flags field are reserved for future use. They MUST be set to zero by clients and ignored by servers and relay agents. Figure 2 gives the format of the 'flags' field.

```
1 1 1 1 1 1
0 1 2 3 4 5 6 7 8 9 0 1 2 3 4 5
+-+-+-+-+-+-+-+-+-+-+-+-+-+-+-+-+
|B|              MBZ             |
+-+-+-+-+-+-+-+-+-+-+-+-+-+-+-+-+

B:   BROADCAST flag
MBZ: MUST BE ZERO (reserved for future use)
```

Figure 2: Format of the 'flags' field

2.1 Configuration parameters repository

The first service provided by DHCP is to provide persistent storage of network parameters for network clients. The model of DHCP persistent storage is that the DHCP service stores a key-value entry for each client, where the key is some unique identifier (for example, an IP subnet number and a unique identifier within the subnet) and the value contains the configuration parameters for the client.

For example, the key might be the pair (IP-subnet-number, hardware-address) (note that the "hardware-address" should be typed by the type of hardware to accommodate possible duplication of hardware addresses resulting from bit-ordering problems in a mixed-media, bridged network) allowing for serial or concurrent reuse of a hardware address on different subnets, and for hardware addresses that may not be globally unique. Alternately, the key might be the pair (IP-subnet-number, hostname), allowing the server to assign parameters intelligently to a DHCP client that has been moved to a different subnet or has changed hardware addresses (perhaps because the network interface failed and was replaced). The protocol defines that the key will be (IP-subnet-number, hardware-address) unless the client explicitly supplies an identifier using the 'client identifier' option. A client can query the DHCP service to retrieve its configuration parameters. The client interface to the configuration parameters repository consists of protocol messages to request configuration parameters and responses from the server carrying the configuration parameters.

2.2 Dynamic allocation of network addresses

The second service provided by DHCP is the allocation of temporary or permanent network (IP) addresses to clients. The basic mechanism for the dynamic allocation of network addresses is simple: a client requests the use of an address for some period of time. The allocation mechanism (the collection of DHCP servers) guarantees not to reallocate that address within the requested time and attempts to return the same network address each time the client requests an address. In this document, the period over which a network address is allocated to a client is referred to as a "lease" [11]. The client may extend its lease with subsequent requests. The client may issue a message to release the address back to the server when the client no longer needs the address. The client may ask for a permanent assignment by asking for an infinite lease. Even when assigning "permanent" addresses, a server may choose to give out lengthy but non-infinite leases to allow detection of the fact that the client has been retired.

In some environments it will be necessary to reassign network addresses due to exhaustion of available addresses. In such environments, the allocation mechanism will reuse addresses whose lease has expired. The server should use whatever information is available in the configuration information repository to choose an address to reuse. For example, the server may choose the least recently assigned address. As a consistency check, the allocating server SHOULD probe the reused address before allocating the address, e.g., with an ICMP echo request, and the client SHOULD probe the newly received address, e.g., with ARP.

3. The Client-Server Protocol

DHCP uses the BOOTP message format defined in RFC 951 and given in table 1 and figure 1. The 'op' field of each DHCP message sent from a client to a server contains BOOTREQUEST. BOOTREPLY is used in the 'op' field of each DHCP message sent from a server to a client.

The first four octets of the 'options' field of the DHCP message contain the (decimal) values 99, 130, 83 and 99, respectively (this is the same magic cookie as is defined in RFC 1497 [17]). The remainder of the 'options' field consists of a list of tagged parameters that are called "options". All of the "vendor extensions" listed in RFC 1497 are also DHCP options. RFC 1533 gives the complete set of options defined for use with DHCP.

Several options have been defined so far. One particular option - the "DHCP message type" option - must be included in every DHCP message. This option defines the "type" of the DHCP message. Additional options may be allowed, required, or not allowed, depending on the DHCP message type.

Throughout this document, DHCP messages that include a 'DHCP message type' option will be referred to by the type of the message; e.g., a DHCP message with 'DHCP message type' option type 1 will be referred to as a "DHCPDISCOVER" message.

3.1 Client-server interaction - allocating a network address

The following summary of the protocol exchanges between clients and servers refers to the DHCP messages described in table 2. The timeline diagram in figure 3 shows the timing relationships in a typical client-server interaction. If the client already knows its address, some steps may be omitted; this abbreviated interaction is described in section 3.2.

1. The client broadcasts a DHCPDISCOVER message on its local physical subnet. The DHCPDISCOVER message MAY include options that suggest values for the network address and lease duration. BOOTP relay agents may pass the message on to DHCP servers not on the same physical subnet.

2. Each server may respond with a DHCPOFFER message that includes an available network address in the 'yiaddr' field (and other configuration parameters in DHCP options). Servers need not reserve the offered network address, although the protocol will work more efficiently if the server avoids allocating the offered network address to another client. When allocating a new address, servers SHOULD check that the offered network address is not already in use; e.g., the server may probe the offered address with an ICMP Echo Request. Servers SHOULD be implemented so that network administrators MAY choose to disable probes of newly allocated addresses. The server transmits the DHCPOFFER message to the client, using the BOOTP relay agent if necessary.

```
Message     Use

-------     ---
```

DHCPDISCOVER   Client broadcast to locate available
                      servers.

DHCPOFFER   Server to client in response to DHCPDISCOVER
                      with offer of configuration parameters.

DHCPREQUEST   Client message to servers either (a)
                      requesting offered parameters from one
                      server and implicitly declining offers from
                      all others, (b) confirming correctness of
                      previously allocated address after, e.g.,
                      system reboot, or (c) extending the lease on
                      a particular network address.

DHCPACK   Server to client with configuration
                      parameters, including committed network
                      address.

DHCPNAK   Server to client indicating client's notion
                      of network address is incorrect (e.g.,
                      client has moved to new subnet) or client's
                      lease as expired

DHCPDECLINE   Client to server indicating network address
                      is already in use.

DHCPRELEASE   Client to server relinquishing network
                      address and cancelling remaining lease.

DHCPINFORM   Client to server, asking only for local
                      configuration parameters; client already has
                      externally configured network address.

Table 2: DHCP messages

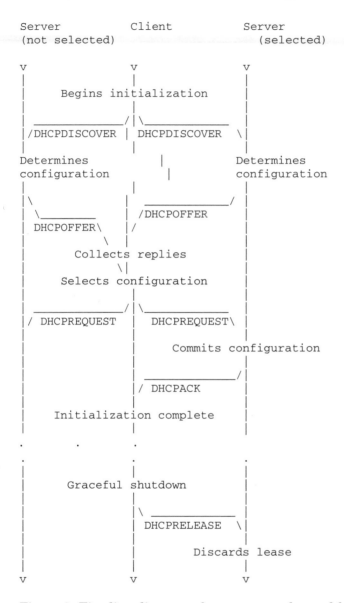

Figure 3: Timeline diagram of messages exchanged between DHCP client and servers when allocating a new network address

3. The client receives one or more DHCPOFFER messages from one or more servers. The client may choose to wait for multiple responses. The client chooses

one server from which to request configuration parameters, based on the config-uration parameters offered in the DHCPOFFER messages. The client broadcasts a DHCPREQUEST message that MUST include the 'server identifier' option to indicate which server it has selected, and that MAY include other options speci-fying desired configuration values. The 'requested IP address' option MUST be set to the value of 'yiaddr' in the DHCPOFFER message from the server. This DHCPREQUEST message is broadcast and relayed through DHCP/BOOTP relay agents. To help ensure that any BOOTP relay agents forward the DHCPREQUEST message to the same set of DHCP servers that received the original DHCPDISCOVER message, the DHCPREQUEST message MUST use the same value in the DHCP message header's 'secs' field and be sent to the same IP broadcast address as the original DHCPDISCOVER message. The client times out and retransmits the DHCPDISCOVER message if the client receives no DHCPOFFER messages.

4. The servers receive the DHCPREQUEST broadcast from the client. Those servers not selected by the DHCPREQUEST message use the message as notification that the client has declined that server's offer. The server selected in the DHCPREQUEST message commits the binding for the client to persistent storage and responds with a DHCPACK message containing the configuration parameters for the requesting client. The combination of 'client identifier' or 'chaddr' and assigned network address constitute a unique identifier for the cli-ent's lease and are used by both the client and server to identify a lease referred to in any DHCP messages. Any configuration parameters in the DHCPACK mes-sage SHOULD NOT conflict with those in the earlier DHCPOFFER message to which the client is responding. The server SHOULD NOT check the offered net-work address at this point. The 'yiaddr' field in the DHCPACK messages is filled in with the selected network address.

If the selected server is unable to satisfy the DHCPREQUEST message (e.g., the requested network address has been allocated), the server SHOULD respond with a DHCPNAK message.

A server MAY choose to mark addresses offered to clients in DHCPOFFER messages as unavailable. The server SHOULD mark an address offered to a cli-ent in a DHCPOFFER message as available if the server receives no DHCPRE-QUEST message from that client.

5. The client receives the DHCPACK message with configuration parame-ters. The client SHOULD perform a final check on the parameters (e.g., ARP for allocated network address), and notes the duration of the lease specified in the DHCPACK message. At this point, the client is configured. If the client detects that the address is already in use (e.g., through the use of ARP), the client MUST send a DHCPDECLINE message to the server and restarts the configuration process. The client SHOULD wait a minimum of ten seconds before restarting the configuration process to avoid excessive network traffic in case of looping.

If the client receives a DHCPNAK message, the client restarts the configuration process.

The client times out and retransmits the DHCPREQUEST message if the client receives neither a DHCPACK or a DHCPNAK message. The client retransmits the DHCPREQUEST according to the retransmission algorithm in section 4.1. The client should choose to retransmit the DHCPREQUEST enough times to give adequate probability of contacting the server without causing the client (and the user of that client) to wait overly long before giving up; e.g., a client retransmitting as described in section 4.1 might retransmit the DHCPREQUEST message four times, for a total delay of 60 seconds, before restarting the initialization procedure. If the client receives neither a DHCPACK or a DHCPNAK message after employing the retransmission algorithm, the client reverts to INIT state and restarts the initialization process. The client SHOULD notify the user that the initialization process has failed and is restarting.

6. The client may choose to relinquish its lease on a network address by sending a DHCPRELEASE message to the server. The client identifies the lease to be released with its 'client identifier', or 'chaddr' and network address in the DHCPRELEASE message. If the client used a 'client identifier' when it obtained the lease, it MUST use the same 'client identifier' in the DHCPRELEASE message.

3.2 Client-server interaction - reusing a previously allocated network address

If a client remembers and wishes to reuse a previously allocated network address, a client may choose to omit some of the steps described in the previous section. The timeline diagram in figure 4 shows the timing relationships in a typical client-server interaction for a client reusing a previously allocated network address.

1. The client broadcasts a DHCPREQUEST message on its local subnet. The message includes the client's network address in the 'requested IP address' option. As the client has not received its network address, it MUST NOT fill in the 'ciaddr' field. BOOTP relay agents pass the message on to DHCP servers not on the same subnet. If the client used a 'client identifier' to obtain its address, the client MUST use the same 'client identifier' in the DHCPREQUEST message.

2. Servers with knowledge of the client's configuration parameters respond with a DHCPACK message to the client. Servers SHOULD NOT check that the client's network address is already in use; the client may respond to ICMP Echo Request messages at this point.

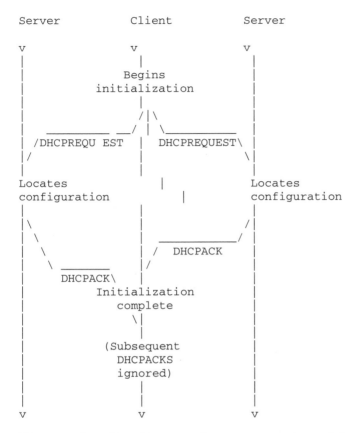

Figure 4: Timeline diagram of messages exchanged between DHCP client and servers when reusing a previously allocated network address

If the client's request is invalid (e.g., the client has moved to a new subnet), servers SHOULD respond with a DHCPNAK message to the client. Servers SHOULD NOT respond if their information is not guaranteed to be accurate. For example, a server that identifies a request for an expired binding that is owned by another server SHOULD NOT respond with a DHCPNAK unless the servers are using an explicit mechanism to maintain coherency among the servers.

If 'giaddr' is 0x0 in the DHCPREQUEST message, the client is on the same subnet as the server. The server MUST broadcast the DHCPNAK message to the 0xffffffff broadcast address because the client may not have a correct network address or subnet mask, and the client may not be answering ARP requests. Otherwise, the server MUST send the DHCPNAK message to the IP address of the BOOTP relay agent, as recorded in 'giaddr'. The relay agent will, in turn, forward the message directly to the client's hardware address, so that the DHCP-NAK can be delivered even if the client has moved to a new network.

3. The client receives the DHCPACK message with configuration parameters. The client performs a final check on the parameters (as in section 3.1), and notes the duration of the lease specified in the DHCPACK message. The specific

lease is implicitly identified by the 'client identifier' or 'chaddr' and the network address. At this point, the client is configured.

If the client detects that the IP address in the DHCPACK message is already in use, the client MUST send a DHCPDECLINE message to the server and restarts the configuration process by requesting a new network address. This action corresponds to the client moving to the INIT state in the DHCP state diagram, which is described in section 4.4.

If the client receives a DHCPNAK message, it cannot reuse its remembered network address. It must instead request a new address by restarting the configuration process, this time using the (non-abbreviated) procedure described in section 3.1. This action also corresponds to the client moving to the INIT state in the DHCP state diagram.

The client times out and retransmits the DHCPREQUEST message if the client receives neither a DHCPACK nor a DHCPNAK message. The client retransmits the DHCPREQUEST according to the retransmission algorithm in section 4.1. The client should choose to retransmit the DHCPREQUEST enough times to give adequate probability of contacting the server without causing the client (and the user of that client) to wait overly long before giving up; e.g., a client retransmitting as described in section 4.1 might retransmit the DHCPREQUEST message four times, for a total delay of 60 seconds, before restarting the initialization procedure. If the client receives neither a DHCPACK or a DHCPNAK message after employing the retransmission algorithm, the client MAY choose to use the previously allocated network address and configuration parameters for the remainder of the unexpired lease. This corresponds to moving to BOUND state in the client state transition diagram shown in figure 5.

4. The client may choose to relinquish its lease on a network address by sending a DHCPRELEASE message to the server. The client identifies the lease to be released with its 'client identifier', or 'chaddr' and network address in the DHCPRELEASE message.

Note that in this case, where the client retains its network address locally, the client will not normally relinquish its lease during a graceful shutdown. Only in the case where the client explicitly needs to relinquish its lease, e.g., the client is about to be moved to a different subnet, will the client send a DHCPRELEASE message.

3.3 Interpretation and representation of time values

A client acquires a lease for a network address for a fixed period of time (which may be infinite). Throughout the protocol, times are to be represented in units of seconds. The time value of 0xffffffff is reserved to represent "infinity".

As clients and servers may not have synchronized clocks, times are represented in DHCP messages as relative times, to be interpreted with respect to the client's local clock. Representing relative times in units of seconds in an unsigned 32 bit word gives a range of relative times from 0 to approximately 100 years, which is sufficient for the relative times to be measured using DHCP.

The algorithm for lease duration interpretation given in the previous paragraph assumes that client and server clocks are stable relative to each other. If there is drift between the two clocks, the server may consider the lease expired before the client does. To compensate, the server may return a shorter lease duration to the client than the server commits to its local database of client information.

3.4 Obtaining parameters with externally configured network address

If a client has obtained a network address through some other means (e.g., manual configuration), it may use a DHCPINFORM request message to obtain other local configuration parameters. Servers receiving a DHCPINFORM message construct a DHCPACK message with any local configuration parameters appropriate for the client without: allocating a new address, checking for an existing binding, filling in 'yiaddr' or including lease time parameters. The servers SHOULD unicast the DHCPACK reply to the address given in the 'ciaddr' field of the DHCPINFORM message.

The server SHOULD check the network address in a DHCPINFORM message for consistency, but MUST NOT check for an existing lease. The server forms a DHCPACK message containing the configuration parameters for the requesting client and sends the DHCPACK message directly to the client.

3.5 Client parameters in DHCP

Not all clients require initialization of all parameters listed in Appendix A. Two techniques are used to reduce the number of parameters transmitted from the server to the client. First, most of the parameters have defaults defined in the Host Requirements RFCs; if the client receives no parameters from the server that override the defaults, a client uses those default values. Second, in its initial DHCPDISCOVER or DHCPREQUEST message, a client may provide the server with a list of specific parameters the client is interested in. If the client includes a list of parameters in a DHCPDISCOVER message, it MUST include that list in any subsequent DHCPREQUEST messages.

The client SHOULD include the 'maximum DHCP message size' option to let the server know how large the server may make its DHCP messages.

The parameters returned to a client may still exceed the space allocated to options in a DHCP message. In this case, two additional options flags (which must appear in the 'options' field of the message) indicate that the 'file' and 'sname' fields are to be used for options.

The client can inform the server which configuration parameters the client is interested in by including the 'parameter request list' option. The data portion of this option explicitly lists the options requested by tag number.

In addition, the client may suggest values for the network address and lease time in the DHCPDISCOVER message. The client may include the 'requested IP address' option to suggest that a particular IP address be assigned, and may include the 'IP address lease time' option to suggest the lease time it would like. Other options representing "hints" at configuration parameters are allowed in a DHCPDISCOVER or DHCPREQUEST message. However, additional options may be ignored by servers, and multiple servers may, therefore, not return identical values for some options. The 'requested IP address' option is to be filled in only in a DHCPREQUEST message when the client is verifying network parameters obtained previously. The client fills in the 'ciaddr' field only when correctly configured with an IP address in BOUND, RENEWING or REBINDING state.

If a server receives a DHCPREQUEST message with an invalid 'requested IP address', the server SHOULD respond to the client with a DHCPNAK message and may choose to report the problem to the system administrator. The server may include an error message in the 'message' option.

3.6 Use of DHCP in clients with multiple interfaces

A client with multiple network interfaces must use DHCP through each interface independently to obtain configuration information parameters for those separate interfaces.

3.7 When clients should use DHCP

A client SHOULD use DHCP to reacquire or verify its IP address and network parameters whenever the local network parameters may have changed; e.g., at system boot time or after a disconnection from the local network, as the local network configuration may change without the client's or user's knowledge.

If a client has knowledge of a previous network address and is unable to contact a local DHCP server, the client may continue to use the previous network address until the lease for that address expires. If the lease expires before the client can contact a DHCP server, the client must immediately discontinue use of the previous network address and may inform local users of the problem.

4. Specification of the DHCP client-server protocol

In this section, we assume that a DHCP server has a block of network addresses from which it can satisfy requests for new addresses. Each server also maintains a database of allocated addresses and leases in local permanent storage.

4.1 Constructing and sending DHCP messages

DHCP clients and servers both construct DHCP messages by filling in fields in the fixed format section of the message and appending tagged data items in the variable length option area. The options area includes first a four-octet 'magic cookie' (which was described in section 3), followed by the options. The last option must always be the 'end' option.

DHCP uses UDP as its transport protocol. DHCP messages from a client to a server are sent to the 'DHCP server' port (67), and DHCP messages from a server to a client are sent to the 'DHCP client' port (68). A server with multiple network address (e.g., a multi-homed host) MAY use any of its network addresses in outgoing DHCP messages.

The 'server identifier' field is used both to identify a DHCP server in a DHCP message and as a destination address from clients to servers. A server with multiple network addresses MUST be prepared to to accept any of its network addresses as identifying that server in a DHCP message. To accommodate potentially incomplete network connectivity, a server MUST choose an address as a 'server identifier' that, to the best of the server's knowledge, is reachable from the client. For example, if the DHCP server and the DHCP client are connected to the same subnet (i.e., the 'giaddr' field in the message from the client is zero), the server SHOULD select the IP address the server is using for communication on that subnet as the 'server identifier'. If the server is using multiple IP addresses on that subnet, any such address may be used. If the server has received a message through a DHCP relay agent, the server SHOULD choose an address from the interface on which the message was recieved as the 'server identifier' (unless the server has other, better information on which to make its choice). DHCP clients MUST use the IP address provided in the 'server identifier' option for any unicast requests to the DHCP server.

DHCP messages broadcast by a client prior to that client obtaining its IP address must have the source address field in the IP header set to 0.

If the 'giaddr' field in a DHCP message from a client is non-zero, the server sends any return messages to the 'DHCP server' port on the BOOTP relay agent whose address appears in 'giaddr'. If the 'giaddr' field is zero and the 'ciaddr' field is nonzero, then the server unicasts DHCPOFFER and DHCPACK messages to the address in 'ciaddr'. If 'giaddr' is zero and 'ciaddr' is zero, and the broadcast bit is set, then the server broadcasts DHCPOFFER and DHCPACK messages to 0xffffffff. If the broadcast bit is not set and 'giaddr' is zero and 'ciaddr' is zero, then the server unicasts DHCPOFFER and DHCPACK messages to the client's hardware address and 'yiaddr' address. In all cases, when 'giaddr' is zero, the server broadcasts any DHCPNAK messages to 0xffffffff.

If the options in a DHCP message extend into the 'sname' and 'file' fields, the 'option overload' option MUST appear in the 'options' field, with value 1, 2 or 3, as specified in RFC 1533. If the 'option overload' option is present in the 'options' field, the options in the 'options' field MUST be terminated by an 'end' option, and MAY contain one or more 'pad' options to fill the options field. The options in the 'sname' and 'file' fields (if in use as indicated by the 'options over load' option) MUST begin with the first octet of the field, MUST be terminated by an 'end' option, and MUST be followed by 'pad' options to fill the remainder of the field. Any individual option in the 'options', 'sname' and 'file' fields MUST be entirely contained in that field. The options in the 'options' field MUST be interpreted first, so that any 'option overload' options may be interpreted. The 'file' field MUST be interpreted next (if the 'option overload' option indicates that the 'file' field contains DHCP options), followed by the 'sname' field.

The values to be passed in an 'option' tag may be too long to fit in the 255 octets available to a single option (e.g., a list of routers in a 'router' option [21]). Options may appear only once, unless otherwise specified in the options document. The client concatenates the values of multiple instances of the same option into a single parameter list for configuration.

DHCP clients are responsible for all message retransmission. The client MUST adopt a retransmission strategy that incorporates a randomized exponential backoff algorithm to determine the delay between retransmissions. The delay between retransmissions SHOULD be chosen to allow sufficient time for replies from the server to be delivered based on the characteristics of the inter network between the client and the server. For example, in a 10Mb/sec Ethernet internetwork, the delay before the first retransmission SHOULD be 4 seconds randomized by the value of a uniform random number chosen from the range -1 to +1. Clients with clocks that provide resolution granularity of less than one second may choose a non-integer randomization value. The delay before the next retransmission SHOULD be 8 seconds randomized by the value of a uniform number chosen from the range -1 to +1. The retransmission delay SHOULD be doubled with subsequent retransmissions up to a maximum of 64 seconds. The client MAY provide an indication of retransmission attempts to the user as an indication of the progress of the configuration process.

The 'xid' field is used by the client to match incoming DHCP messages with pending requests. A DHCP client MUST choose 'xid's in such a way as to minimize the chance of using an 'xid' identical to one used by another client. For example, a client may choose a different, random initial 'xid' each time the client is rebooted, and subsequently use sequential 'xid's until the next reboot. Selecting a new 'xid' for each retransmission is an implementation decision. A client may choose to reuse the same 'xid' or select a new 'xid' for each retransmitted message.

Normally, DHCP servers and BOOTP relay agents attempt to deliver DHCPOFFER, DHCPACK and DHCPNAK messages directly to the client using uicast delivery. The IP destination address (in the IP header) is set to the DHCP 'yiaddr' address and the link-layer destination address is set to the DHCP 'chaddr' address. Unfortunately, some client implementations are unable to receive such unicast IP datagrams until the implementation has been configured with a valid IP address (leading to a deadlock in which the client's IP address cannot be delivered until the client has been configured with an IP address).

A client that cannot receive unicast IP datagrams until its protocol software has been configured with an IP address SHOULD set the BROADCAST bit in the 'flags' field to 1 in any DHCPDISCOVER or DHCPREQUEST messages that client sends. The BROADCAST bit will provide a hint to the DHCP server and BOOTP relay agent to broadcast any messages to the client on the client's subnet. A client that can receive unicast IP datagrams before its protocol software has been configured SHOULD clear the BROADCAST bit to 0. The BOOTP clarifications document discusses the ramifications of the use of the BROADCAST bit [21].

A server or relay agent sending or relaying a DHCP message directly to a DHCP client (i.e., not to a relay agent specified in the 'giaddr' field) SHOULD examine the BROADCAST bit in the 'flags' field. If this bit is set to 1, the DHCP message SHOULD be sent as an IP broadcast using an IP broadcast address (preferably 0xffffffff) as the IP destination address and the link-layer broadcast address as the link-layer destination address. If the BROADCAST bit is cleared to 0, the message SHOULD be sent as an IP unicast to the IP address specified in the 'yiaddr' field and the link-layer address specified in the 'chaddr' field. If unicasting is not possible, the message MAY be sent as an IP broadcast using an IP broadcast address (preferably 0xffffffff) as the IP destination address and the link- layer broadcast address as the link-layer destination address.

4.2 DHCP server administrative controls

DHCP servers are not required to respond to every DHCPDISCOVER and DHCPREQUEST message they receive. For example, a network administrator, to retain stringent control over the clients attached to the network, may choose to configure DHCP servers to respond only to clients that have been previously registered through some external mechanism. The DHCP specification describes only the interactions between clients and servers when the clients and servers choose to interact; it is beyond the scope of the DHCP specification to describe all of the administrative controls that system administrators might want to use. Specific DHCP server implementations may incorporate any controls or policies desired by a network administrator.

In some environments, a DHCP server will have to consider the values of the vendor class options included in DHCPDISCOVER or DHCPREQUEST messages when determining the correct parameters for a particular client.

A DHCP server needs to use some unique identifier to associate a client with its lease. The client MAY choose to explicitly provide the identifier through the 'client identifier' option. If the client supplies a 'client identifier', the client MUST use the same 'client identifier' in all subsequent messages, and the server MUST use that identifier to identify the client. If the client does not provide a 'client identifier' option, the server MUST use the contents of the 'chaddr' field to identify the client. It is crucial for a DHCP client to use an identifier unique within the subnet to which the client is attached in the 'client identifier' option. Use of 'chaddr' as the client's unique identifier may cause unexpected results, as that identifier may be associated with a hardware interface that could be moved to a new client. Some sites may choose to use a manufacturer's serial number as the 'client identifier', to avoid unexpected changes in a clients network address due to transfer of hardware interfaces among computers. Sites may also choose to use a DNS name as the 'client identifier', causing address leases to be associated with the DNS name rather than a specific hardware box.

DHCP clients are free to use any strategy in selecting a DHCP server among those from which the client receives a DHCPOFFER message. The client implementation of DHCP SHOULD provide a mechanism for the user to select directly the 'vendor class identifier' values.

4.3 DHCP server behavior

A DHCP server processes incoming DHCP messages from a client based on the current state of the binding for that client. A DHCP server can receive the following messages from a client:

- DHCPDISCOVER
- DHCPREQUEST
- DHCPDECLINE
- DHCPRELEASE
- DHCPINFORM

Table 3 gives the use of the fields and options in a DHCP message by a server. The remainder of this section describes the action of the DHCP server for each possible incoming message.

4.3.1 DHCPDISCOVER message

When a server receives a DHCPDISCOVER message from a client, the server chooses a network address for the requesting client. If no address is available, the server may choose to report the problem to the system administrator. If an address is available, the new address SHOULD be chosen as follows:

- The client's current address as recorded in the client's current binding, ELSE
- The client's previous address as recorded in the client's (now expired or released) binding, if that address is in the server's pool of available addresses and not already allocated, ELSE
- The address requested in the 'Requested IP Address' option, if that address is valid and not already allocated, ELSE
- A new address allocated from the server's pool of available addresses; the address is selected based on the subnet from which the message was received (if 'giaddr' is 0) or on the address of the relay agent that forwarded the message ('giaddr' when not 0).

As described in section 4.2, a server MAY, for administrative reasons, assign an address other than the one requested, or may refuse to allocate an address to a particular client even though free addresses are available.

Note that, in some network architectures (e.g., internets with more than one IP subnet assigned to a physical network segment), it may be the case that the DHCP client should be assigned an address from a different subnet than the address recorded in 'giaddr'. Thus, DHCP does not require that the client be assigned as address from the subnet in 'giaddr'. A server is free to choose some other subnet, and it is beyond the scope of the DHCP specification to describe ways in which the assigned IP address might be chosen.

While not required for correct operation of DHCP, the server SHOULD NOT reuse the selected network address before the client responds to the server's DHCPOFFER message. The server may choose to record the address as offered to the client.

The server must also choose an expiration time for the lease, as follows:

- IF the client has not requested a specific lease in the DHCPDISCOVER message and the client already has an assigned network address, the server returns the lease expiration time previously assigned to that address (note that the client must explicitly request a specific lease to extend the expiration time on a previously assigned address), ELSE
- IF the client has not requested a specific lease in the DHCPDISCOVER message and the client does not have an assigned network address, the server assigns a locally configured default lease time, ELSE

- IF the client has requested a specific lease in the DHCPDISCOVER message (regardless of whether the client has an assigned network address), the server may choose either to return the requested lease (if the lease is acceptable to local policy) or select another lease.

Field	DHCPOFFER	DHCPACK	DHCPNAK
`op`	BOOTREPLY	BOOTREPLY	BOOTREPLY
`htype`	(From "Assigned Numbers" RFC)		
`hlen`	(Hardware address length in octets)		
`hops`	0	0	0
`xid`	`xid` from client DHCPDISCOVER message	`xid` from client DHCPREQUEST message	`xid` from client DHCPREQUEST message
`secs`	0	0	0
`ciaddr`	0	`ciaddr` from DHCPREQUEST or 0	0
`yiaddr`	IP address offered to client	IP address assigned to client	0
`siaddr`	IP address of next bootstrap server	IP address of next bootstrap server	0
`flags`	`flags` from client DHCPDISCOVER message	`flags` from client DHCPREQUEST message	`flags` from client DHCPREQUEST message
`giaddr`	`giaddr` from client DHCPDISCOVER message	`giaddr` from client DHCPREQUEST message	`giaddr` from client DHCPREQUEST message
`chaddr`	`chaddr` from client DHCPDISCOVER message	`chaddr` from client DHCPREQUEST message	`chaddr` from client DHCPREQUEST message
`sname`	Server host name or options	Server host name or options	(unused)
`file`	Client boot file name or options	Client boot file name or options	(unused)
`options`	options	options	

```
Option                          DHCPOFFER  DHCPACK            DHCPNAK
------                          ---------  -------            -------
Requested IP address            MUST NOT   MUST NOT           MUST NOT
IP address lease time           MUST       MUST (DHCPREQUEST) MUST NOT
                                           MUST NOT (DHCPINFORM)
Use 'file'/'sname' fields       MAY        MAY                MUST NOT
DHCP message type               DHCPOFFER  DHCPACK            DHCPNAK
Parameter request list          MUST NOT   MUST NOT           MUST NOT
Message                         SHOULD     SHOULD             SHOULD
Client identifier               MUST NOT   MUST NOT           MAY
Vendor class identifier         MAY        MAY                MAY
Server identifier               MUST       MUST               MUST
Maximum message size            MUST NOT   MUST NOT           MUST NOT
All others                      MAY        MAY                MUST NOT
```

Table 3: Fields and options used by DHCP servers

Once the network address and lease have been determined, the server constructs a DHCPOFFER message with the offered configuration parameters. It is important for all DHCP servers to return the same parameters (with the possible exception of a newly allocated network address) to ensure predictable client behavior regardless of which server the client selects. The configuration parameters MUST be selected by applying the following rules in the order given below. The network administrator is responsible for configuring multiple DHCP servers to ensure uniform responses from those servers. The server MUST return to the client:

- The client's network address, as determined by the rules given earlier in this section,
- The expiration time for the client's lease, as determined by the rules given earlier in this section,
- Parameters requested by the client, according to the following rules:

— IF the server has been explicitly configured with a default value for the parameter, the server MUST include that value in an appropriate option in the 'option' field, ELSE

— IF the server recognizes the parameter as a parameter defined in the Host Requirements Document, the server MUST include the default value for that parameter as given in the Host Requirements Document in an appropriate option in the 'option' field, ELSE

— The server MUST NOT return a value for that parameter, The server MUST supply as many of the requested parameters as possible and MUST omit any parameters it cannot provide. The server MUST include each requested parameter only once unless explicitly allowed in the DHCP Options and BOOTP Vendor Extensions document.

- Any parameters from the existing binding that differ from the Host Requirements Document defaults,
- Any parameters specific to this client (as identified by the contents of 'chaddr' or 'client identifier' in the DHCPDISCOVER or DHCPREQUEST message), e.g., as configured by the network administrator,

- Any parameters specific to this client's class (as identified by the contents of the 'vendor class identifier' option in the DHCPDISCOVER or DHCPRE-QUEST message), e.g., as configured by the network administrator; the parameters MUST be identified by an exact match between the client's vendor class identifiers and the client's classes identified in the server,

- Parameters with non-default values on the client's subnet.

The server MAY choose to return the 'vendor class identifier' used to determine the parameters in the DHCPOFFER message to assist the client in selecting which DHCPOFFER to accept. The server inserts the 'xid' field from the DHCPDISCOVER message into the 'xid' field of the DHCPOFFER message and sends the DHCPOFFER message to the requesting client.

4.3.2 DHCPREQUEST message

A DHCPREQUEST message may come from a client responding to a DHCPOFFER message from a server, from a client verifying a previously allocated IP address or from a client extending the lease on a network address. If the DHCPREQUEST message contains a 'server identifier' option, the message is in response to a DHCPOFFER message. Otherwise, the message is a request to verify or extend an existing lease. If the client uses a 'client identifier' in a DHCPREQUEST message, it MUST use that same 'client identifier' in all subsequent messages. If the client included a list of requested parameters in a DHCP-DISCOVER message, it MUST include that list in all subsequent messages.

Any configuration parameters in the DHCPACK message SHOULD NOT conflict with those in the earlier DHCPOFFER message to which the client is responding. The client SHOULD use the parameters in the DHCPACK message for configuration.

Clients send DHCPREQUEST messages as follows:

- DHCPREQUEST generated during SELECTING state:

  Client inserts the address of the selected server in 'server identifier', 'ciaddr' MUST be zero, 'requested IP address' MUST be filled in with the yiaddr value from the chosen DHCPOFFER.

  Note that the client may choose to collect several DHCPOFFER messages and select the "best" offer. The client indicates its selection by identifying the offering server in the DHCPREQUEST message. If the client receives no acceptable offers, the client may choose to try another DHCPDISCOVER message. Therefore, the servers may not receive a specific DHCPREQUEST from which they can decide whether or not the client has accepted the offer. Because the servers have not committed any network address assignments on the basis of a DHCPOFFER, servers are free to reuse offered network addresses in response to subsequent requests. As an implementation detail, servers SHOULD NOT reuse offered addresses and may use an implementation-specific timeout mechanism to decide when to reuse an offered address.

- DHCPREQUEST generated during INIT-REBOOT state:

'server identifier' MUST NOT be filled in, 'requested IP address' option MUST be filled in with client's notion of its previously assigned address. 'ciaddr' MUST be zero. The client is seeking to verify a previously allocated, cached configuration. Server SHOULD send a DHCPNAK message to the client if the 'requested IP address' is incorrect, or is on the wrong network.

Determining whether a client in the INIT-REBOOT state is on the correct network is done by examining the contents of 'giaddr', the 'requested IP address' option, and a database lookup. If the DHCP server detects that the client is on the wrong net (i.e., the result of applying the local subnet mask or remote subnet mask (if 'giaddr' is not zero) to 'requested IP address' option value doesn't match reality), then the server SHOULD send a DHCP-NAK message to the client.

If the network is correct, then the DHCP server should check if the client's notion of its IP address is correct. If not, then the server SHOULD send a DHCPNAK message to the client. If the DHCP server has no record of this client, then it MUST remain silent, and MAY output a warning to the network administrator. This behavior is necessary for peaceful coexistence of non-communicating DHCP servers on the same wire.

If 'giaddr' is 0x0 in the DHCPREQUEST message, the client is on the same subnet as the server. The server MUST broadcast the DHCPNAK message to the 0xffffffff broadcast address because the client may not have a correct network address or subnet mask, and the client may not be answering ARP requests.

If 'giaddr' is set in the DHCPREQUEST message, the client is on a different subnet. The server MUST set the broadcast bit in the DHCPNAK, so that the relay agent will broadcast the DHCPNAK to the client, because the client may not have a correct network address or subnet mask, and the client may not be answering ARP requests.

- DHCPREQUEST generated during RENEWING state:

'server identifier' MUST NOT be filled in, 'requested IP address' option MUST NOT be filled in, 'ciaddr' MUST be filled in with client's IP address. In this situation, the client is completely configured, and is trying to extend its lease. This message will be unicast, so no relay agents will be involved in its transmission. Because 'giaddr' is therefore not filled in, the DHCP server will trust the value in 'ciaddr', and use it when replying to the client.

A client MAY choose to renew or extend its lease prior to T1. The server may choose not to extend the lease (as a policy decision by the network administrator), but should return a DHCPACK message regardless.

- DHCPREQUEST generated during REBINDING state:

'server identifier' MUST NOT be filled in, 'requested IP address' option MUST NOT be filled in, 'ciaddr' MUST be filled in with client's IP address.

In this situation, the client is completely configured, and is trying to extend its lease. This message MUST be broadcast to the 0xffffffff IP broadcast address. The DHCP server SHOULD check 'ciaddr' for correctness before replying to the DHCPREQUEST.

The DHCPREQUEST from a REBINDING client is intended to accommodate sites that have multiple DHCP servers and a mechanism for maintaining consistency among leases managed by multiple servers. A DHCP server MAY extend a client's lease only if it has local administrative authority to do so.

4.3.3 DHCPDECLINE message

If the server receives a DHCPDECLINE message, the client has discovered through some other means that the suggested network address is already in use. The server MUST mark the network address as not available and SHOULD notify the local system administrator of a possible configuration problem.

4.3.4 DHCPRELEASE message

Upon receipt of a DHCPRELEASE message, the server marks the network address as not allocated. The server SHOULD retain a record of the client's initialization parameters for possible reuse in response to subsequent requests from the client.

4.3.5 DHCPINFORM message

The server responds to a DHCPINFORM message by sending a DHCPACK message directly to the address given in the 'ciaddr' field of the DHCPINFORM message. The server MUST NOT send a lease expiration time to the client and SHOULD NOT fill in 'yiaddr'. The server includes other parameters in the DHC-PACK message as defined in section 4.3.1.

4.3.6 Client messages

Table 4 details the differences between messages from clients in various states.

```
--------------------------------------------------------------------
|              |INIT-REBOOT  |SELECTING    |RENEWING     |REBINDING  |
--------------------------------------------------------------------
|broad/unicast |broadcast    |broadcast    |unicast      |broadcast  |
|server-ip     |MUST NOT     |MUST         |MUST NOT     |MUST NOT   |
|requested-ip  |MUST         |MUST         |MUST NOT     |MUST NOT   |
|ciaddr        |zero         |zero         |IP address   |IP address |
--------------------------------------------------------------------
```

Table 4: Client messages from different states

4.4 DHCP client behavior

Figure 5 gives a state-transition diagram for a DHCP client. A client can receive the following messages from a server:

- DHCPOFFER
- DHCPACK
- DHCPNAK

The DHCPINFORM message is not shown in figure 5. A client simply sends the DHCPINFORM and waits for DHCPACK messages. Once the client has selected its parameters, it has completed the configuration process.

Table 5 gives the use of the fields and options in a DHCP message by a client. The remainder of this section describes the action of the DHCP client for each possible incoming message. The description in the following section corresponds to the full configuration procedure previously described in section 3.1, and the text in the subsequent section corresponds to the abbreviated configuration procedure described in section 3.2.

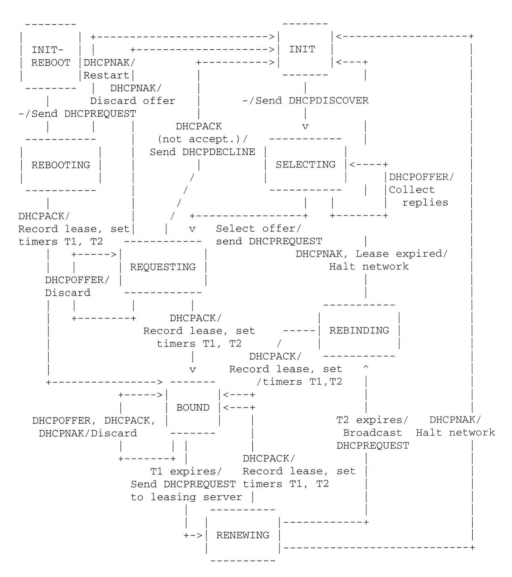

Figure 5: State-transition diagram for DHCP clients

4.4.1 Initialization and allocation of network address

The client begins in INIT state and forms a DHCPDISCOVER message. The client SHOULD wait a random time between one and ten seconds to desynchronize the use of DHCP at startup. The client sets 'ciaddr' to 0x00000000. The client MAY request specific parameters by including the 'parameter request list' option. The client MAY suggest a network address and/or lease time by including the 'requested IP address' and 'IP address lease time' options. The client MUST include its hardware address in the 'chaddr' field, if necessary for delivery of DHCP reply messages. The client MAY include a different unique identifier in the 'client identifier' option, as discussed in section 4.2. If the client included a list of requested parameters in a DHCPDISCOVER message, it MUST include that list in all subsequent messages.

The client generates and records a random transaction identifier and inserts that identifier into the 'xid' field. The client records its own local time for later use in computing the lease expiration. The client then broadcasts the DHCPDISCOVER on the local hardware broadcast address to the 0xffffffff IP broadcast address and 'DHCP server' UDP port.

If the 'xid' of an arriving DHCPOFFER message does not match the 'xid' of the most recent DHCPDISCOVER message, the DHCPOFFER message must be silently discarded. Any arriving DHCPACK messages must be silently discarded.

The client collects DHCPOFFER messages over a period of time, selects one DHCPOFFER message from the (possibly many) incoming DHCPOFFER messages (e.g., the first DHCPOFFER message or the DHCPOFFER message from the previously used server) and extracts the server address from the 'server identifier' option in the DHCPOFFER message. The time over which the client collects messages and the mechanism used to select one DHCPOFFER are implementation dependent.

```
Field        DHCPDISCOVER          DHCPREQUEST          DHCPDECLINE,
             DHCPINFORM                                 DHCPRELEASE
-----        -----------           -----------          -----------
'op'         BOOTREQUEST           BOOTREQUEST          BOOTREQUEST
'htype'      (From "Assigned Numbers" RFC)
'hlen'       (Hardware address length in octets)
'hops'       0                     0                    0
'xid'        selected by client    'xid' from server    selected by
                                   DHCPOFFER message    client
'secs'       0 or seconds since    0 or seconds since   0
             DHCP process started  DHCP process started
'flags'      Set 'BROADCAST'       Set 'BROADCAST'      0
             flag if client        flag if client
             requires broadcast    requires broadcast
             reply                 reply
'ciaddr'     0 (DHCPDISCOVER)      0 or client's        0 (DHCPDECLINE)
             client's              network address      client's network
             network address       (BOUND/RENEW/REBIND) address
             (DHCPINFORM)                               (DHCPRELEASE)
'yiaddr'     0                     0                    0
'siaddr'     0                     0                    0
'giaddr'     0                     0                    0
```

Field	DHCPDISCOVER DHCPINFORM	DHCPREQUEST	DHCPDECLINE, DHCPRELEASE
'chaddr'	client's hardware address	client's hardware address	client's hardware address
'sname'	options, if indicated in 'sname/file' option; otherwise unused	options, if indicated in 'sname/file' option; otherwise unused	(unused)
'file'	options, if indicated in 'sname/file' option; otherwise unused	options, if indicated in 'sname/file' option; otherwise unused	(unused)
'options'	options	options	(unused)

Option	DHCPDISCOVER DHCPINFORM	DHCPREQUEST	DHCPDECLINE, DHCPRELEASE
Requested IP address	MAY (DISCOVER) MUST NOT (INFORM)	MUST (in SELECTING or INIT-REBOOT) MUST NOT (in BOUND or RENEWING)	MUST (DHCPDECLINE), MUST NOT (DHCPRELEASE)
IP address lease time	MAY (DISCOVER) MUST NOT (INFORM)	MAY	MUST NOT
Use 'file'/'sname' fields	MAY	MAY	MAY
DHCP message type	DHCPDISCOVER/ DHCPINFORM	DHCPREQUEST	DHCPDECLINE/ DHCPRELEASE
Client identifier	MAY	MAY	MAY
Vendor class identifier	MAY	MAY	MUST NOT
Server identifier	MUST NOT SELECTING) MUST NOT (after INIT-REBOOT, BOUND, RENEWING or REBINDING)	MUST (after SELECTING)	MUST
Parameter request list	MAY	MAY	MUST NOT
Maximum message size	MAY	MAY	MUST NOT
Message	SHOULD NOT	SHOULD NOT	SHOULD
Site-specific	MAY	MAY	MUST NOT
All others	MAY	MAY	MUST NOT

Table 5: Fields and options used by DHCP clients

If the parameters are acceptable, the client records the address of the server that supplied the parameters from the 'server identifier' field and sends that address in the 'server identifier' field of a DHCPREQUEST broadcast message. Once the DHCPACK message from the server arrives, the client is initialized and moves to BOUND state. The DHCPREQUEST message contains the same 'xid' as the DHCPOFFER message. The client records the lease expiration time as the sum of the time at which the original request was sent and the duration of the lease from the DHCPACK message. The client SHOULD perform a check on the suggested address to ensure that the address is not already in use. For example, if the client is on a network that supports ARP, the client may issue an ARP request for the suggested request. When broadcasting an ARP request for the suggested address, the client must fill in its own hardware address as the sender's hardware address, and 0 as the sender's IP address, to avoid confusing ARP caches in other hosts on the same subnet. If the network address appears to be in use, the client MUST send a DHCPDECLINE message to the server. The client SHOULD broadcast an ARP reply to announce the client's new IP address and clear any outdated ARP cache entries in hosts on the client's subnet.

4.4.2 Initialization with known network address

The client begins in INIT-REBOOT state and sends a DHCPREQUEST message. The client MUST insert its known network address as a 'requested IP address' option in the DHCPREQUEST message. The client may request specific configuration parameters by including the 'parameter request list' option. The client generates and records a random transaction identifier and inserts that identifier into the 'xid' field. The client records its own local time for later use in computing the lease expiration. The client MUST NOT include a 'server identifier' in the DHCPREQUEST message. The client then broadcasts the DHCPREQUEST on the local hardware broadcast address to the 'DHCP server' UDP port.

Once a DHCPACK message with an 'xid' field matching that in the client's DHCPREQUEST message arrives from any server, the client is initialized and moves to BOUND state. The client records the lease expiration time as the sum of the time at which the DHCPREQUEST message was sent and the duration of the lease from the DHCPACK message.

4.4.3 Initialization with an externally assigned network address

The client sends a DHCPINFORM message. The client may request specific configuration parameters by including the 'parameter request list' option. The client generates and records a random transaction identifier and inserts that identifier into the 'xid' field. The client places its own network address in the 'ciaddr' field. The client SHOULD NOT request lease time parameters.

The client then unicasts the DHCPINFORM to the DHCP server if it knows the server's address, otherwise it broadcasts the message to the limited (all 1s) broadcast address. DHCPINFORM messages MUST be directed to the 'DHCP server' UDP port.

Once a DHCPACK message with an 'xid' field matching that in the client's DHCPINFORM message arrives from any server, the client is initialized.

If the client does not receive a DHCPACK within a reasonable period of time (60 seconds or 4 tries if using timeout suggested in section 4.1), then it SHOULD display a message informing the user of the problem, and then SHOULD begin network processing using suitable defaults as per Appendix A.

4.4.4 Use of broadcast and unicast

The DHCP client broadcasts DHCPDISCOVER, DHCPREQUEST and DHCPINFORM messages, unless the client knows the address of a DHCP server. The client unicasts DHCPRELEASE messages to the server. Because the client is declining the use of the IP address supplied by the server, the client broadcasts DHCPDECLINE messages.

When the DHCP client knows the address of a DHCP server, in either INIT or REBOOTING state, the client may use that address in the DHCPDISCOVER or DHCPREQUEST rather than the IP broadcast address.

The client may also use unicast to send DHCPINFORM messages to a known DHCP server. If the client receives no response to DHCP messages sent to the IP address of a known DHCP server, the DHCP client reverts to using the IP broadcast address.

4.4.5 Reacquisition and expiration

The client maintains two times, T1 and T2, that specify the times at which the client tries to extend its lease on its network address. T1 is the time at which the client enters the RENEWING state and attempts to contact the server that originally issued the client's network address. T2 is the time at which the client enters the REBINDING state and attempts to contact any server. T1 MUST be earlier than T2, which, in turn, MUST be earlier than the time at which the client's lease will expire.

To avoid the need for synchronized clocks, T1 and T2 are expressed in options as relative times [2].

At time T1 the client moves to RENEWING state and sends (via unicast) a DHCPREQUEST message to the server to extend its lease. The client sets the 'ciaddr' field in the DHCPREQUEST to its current network address. The client records the local time at which the DHCPREQUEST message is sent for computation of the lease expiration time. The client MUST NOT include a 'server identifier' in the DHCPREQUEST message.

Any DHCPACK messages that arrive with an 'xid' that does not match the 'xid' of the client's DHCPREQUEST message are silently discarded. When the client receives a DHCPACK from the server, the client computes the lease expiration time as the sum of the time at which the client sent the DHCPREQUEST message and the duration of the lease in the DHCPACK message. The client has successfully reacquired its network address, returns to BOUND state and may continue network processing.

If no DHCPACK arrives before time T2, the client moves to REBINDING state and sends (via broadcast) a DHCPREQUEST message to extend its lease. The client sets the 'ciaddr' field in the DHCPREQUEST to its current network address. The client MUST NOT include a 'server identifier' in the DHCPRE-QUEST message.

Times T1 and T2 are configurable by the server through options. T1 defaults to (0.5 * duration_of_lease). T2 defaults to (0.875 * duration_of_lease). Times T1 and T2 SHOULD be chosen with some random "fuzz" around a fixed value, to avoid synchronization of client reacquisition.

A client MAY choose to renew or extend its lease prior to T1. The server MAY choose to extend the client's lease according to policy set by the network administrator. The server SHOULD return T1 and T2, and their values SHOULD be adjusted from their original values to take account of the time remaining on the lease.

In both RENEWING and REBINDING states, if the client receives no response to its DHCPREQUEST message, the client SHOULD wait one-half of the remaining time until T2 (in RENEWING state) and one-half of the remaining lease time (in REBINDING state), down to a minimum of 60 seconds, before retransmitting the DHCPREQUEST message.

If the lease expires before the client receives a DHCPACK, the client moves to INIT state, MUST immediately stop any other network processing and requests network initialization parameters as if the client were uninitialized. If the client then receives a DHCPACK allocating that client its previous network address, the client SHOULD continue network processing. If the client is given a new network address, it MUST NOT continue using the previous network address and SHOULD notify the local users of the problem.

4.4.6 DHCPRELEASE

If the client no longer requires use of its assigned network address (e.g., the client is gracefully shut down), the client sends a DHCPRELEASE message to the server. Note that the correct operation of DHCP does not depend on the transmission of DHCPRELEASE messages.

5. Acknowledgments

The author thanks the many (and too numerous to mention!) members of the DHC WG for their tireless and ongoing efforts in the development of DHCP and this document.

The efforts of J Allard, Mike Carney, Dave Lapp, Fred Lien and John Mendonca in organizing DHCP interoperability testing sessions are gratefully acknowledged.

The development of this document was supported in part by grants from the Corporation for National Research Initiatives (CNRI), Bucknell XSUniversity and Sun Microsystems.

6. References

[1] Acetta, M., "Resource Location Protocol", RFC 887, CMU, December 1983.

[2] Alexander, S., and R. Droms, "DHCP Options and BOOTP Vendor Extensions", RFC 1533, Lachman Technology, Inc., Bucknell University, October 1993.

[3] Braden, R., Editor, "Requirements for Internet Hosts -- Communication Layers", STD 3, RFC 1122, USC/Information Sciences Institute, October 1989.

[4] Braden, R., Editor, "Requirements for Internet Hosts -- Application and Support, STD 3, RFC 1123, USC/Information Sciences Institute, October 1989.

[5] Brownell, D, "Dynamic Reverse Address Resolution Protocol (DRARP)", Work in Progress.

[6] Comer, D., and R. Droms, "Uniform Access to Internet Directory Services", Proc. of ACM SIGCOMM '90 (Special issue of Computer Communications Review), 20(4):50--59, 1990.

[7] Croft, B., and J. Gilmore, "Bootstrap Protocol (BOOTP)", RFC 951, Stanford and SUN Microsystems, September 1985.

[8] Deering, S., "ICMP Router Discovery Messages", RFC 1256, Xerox PARC, September 1991.

[9] Droms, D., "Interoperation between DHCP and BOOTP", RFC 1534, Bucknell University, October 1993.

[10] Finlayson, R., Mann, T., Mogul, J., and M. Theimer, "A Reverse Address Resolution Protocol", RFC 903, Stanford, June 1984.

[11] Gray C., and D. Cheriton, "Leases: An Efficient Fault-Tolerant Mechanism for Distributed File Cache Consistency", In Proc. of the Twelfth ACM Symposium on Operating Systems Design, 1989.

[12] Mockapetris, P., "Domain Names -- Concepts and Facilities", STD 13, RFC 1034, USC/Information Sciences Institute, November 1987.

[13] Mockapetris, P., "Domain Names -- Implementation and Specification", STD 13, RFC 1035, USC/Information Sciences Institute, November 1987.

[14] Mogul J., and S. Deering, "Path MTU Discovery", RFC 1191, November 1990.

[15] Morgan, R., "Dynamic IP Address Assignment for Ethernet Attached Hosts", Work in Progress.

[16] Postel, J., "Internet Control Message Protocol", STD 5, RFC 792, USC/Information Sciences Institute, September 1981.

[17] Reynolds, J., "BOOTP Vendor Information Extensions", RFC 1497, USC/Information Sciences Institute, August 1993.

[18] Reynolds, J., and J. Postel, "Assigned Numbers", STD 2, RFC 1700, USC/Information Sciences Institute, October 1994.

[19] Jeffrey Schiller and Mark Rosenstein. A Protocol for the Dynamic Assignment of IP Addresses for use on an Ethernet. (Available from the Athena Project, MIT), 1989.

[20] Sollins, K., "The TFTP Protocol (Revision 2)", RFC 783, NIC, June 1981.

[21] Wimer, W., "Clarifications and Extensions for the Bootstrap Protocol", RFC 1542, Carnegie Mellon University, October 1993.

7. Security Considerations

DHCP is built directly on UDP and IP which are as yet inherently insecure. Furthermore, DHCP is generally intended to make maintenance of remote and/or diskless hosts easier. While perhaps not impossible, configuring such hosts with passwords or keys may be difficult and inconvenient. Therefore, DHCP in its current form is quite insecure.

Unauthorized DHCP servers may be easily set up. Such servers can then send false and potentially disruptive information to clients such as incorrect or duplicate IP addresses, incorrect routing information (including spoof routers, etc.), incorrect domain nameserver addresses (such as spoof nameservers), and so on. Clearly, once this seed information is in place, an attacker can further compromise affected systems.

Malicious DHCP clients could masquerade as legitimate clients and retrieve information intended for those legitimate clients. Where dynamic allocation of resources is used, a malicious client could claim all resources for itself, thereby denying resources to legitimate clients.

8. Author's Address

Ralph Droms
Computer Science Department
323 Dana Engineering
Bucknell University
Lewisburg, PA 17837

Phone: (717) 524-1145
EMail: droms@bucknell.edu

A. Host Configuration Parameters

```
IP-layer_parameters,_per_host:_

Be a router                    on/off                     HRC 3.1
Non-local source routing       on/off                     HRC 3.3.5
Policy filters for
non-local source routing       (list)                     HRC 3.3.5
Maximum reassembly size        integer                    HRC 3.3.2
Default TTL                    integer                    HRC 3.2.1.7
PMTU aging timeout             integer                    MTU 6.6
MTU plateau table              (list)                     MTU 7
IP-layer_parameters,_per_interface:_
IP address                     (address)                  HRC 3.3.1.6
Subnet mask                    (address mask)             HRC 3.3.1.6
MTU                            integer                    HRC 3.3.3
All-subnets-MTU                on/off                     HRC 3.3.3
Broadcast address flavor       0x00000000/0xffffffff      HRC 3.3.6
Perform mask discovery         on/off                     HRC 3.2.2.9
Be a mask supplier             on/off                     HRC 3.2.2.9
Perform router discovery       on/off                     RD 5.1
Router solicitation address    (address)                  RD 5.1
Default routers, list of:
        router address         (address)                  HRC 3.3.1.6
        preference level       integer                    HRC 3.3.1.6
Static routes, list of:
        destination            (host/subnet/net)          HRC 3.3.1.2
        destination mask       (address mask)             HRC 3.3.1.2
        type-of-service        integer                    HRC 3.3.1.2
        first-hop router       (address)                  HRC 3.3.1.2
        ignore redirects       on/off                     HRC 3.3.1.2
        PMTU                   integer                    MTU 6.6
        perform PMTU discovery on/off                     MTU 6.6


Link-layer_parameters,_per_interface:_
Trailers                       on/off                     HRC 2.3.1
ARP cache timeout              integer                    HRC 2.3.2.1
Ethernet encapsulation         (RFC 894/RFC 1042)         HRC 2.3.3


TCP_parameters,_per_host:_
TTL                            integer                    HRC 4.2.2.19
Keep-alive interval            integer                    HRC 4.2.3.6
Keep-alive data size           0/1                        HRC 4.2.3.6

Key:

    MTU = Path MTU Discovery (RFC 1191, Proposed Standard)
    RD = Router Discovery (RFC 1256, Proposed Standard)
```

Glossary

address pool—the set of IP addresses available for assignment by a DHCP server.

address resolution protocol—a protocol whereby a computer knowing only the IP address of another machine can learn its Ethernet address.

ARP—see *address resolution protocol*.

backoff—increasing time between retransmissions to avoid network congestion.

binding—correspondence between an IP address and a DHCP client. See also *lease*.

boot—of a computer, to initialize and load the operating system.

BOOTP—see *bootstrap protocol*.

bootstrap protocol—a way for a booting computer to find out its IP address and the location of the boot file with the rest of its parameters.

bridge—a machine that connects two network segments together without routing.

byte order—whether large units of information are transmitted on a network most significant byte first, or least significant byte first.

checksum—the result of a mathematical function applied to a packet and transmitted with the packet. It helps to detect transmission errors.

chicken-and-egg problems—which came first? A computer cannot contact a server for its address and parameters until it has an address. Solved by BOOTP and later DHCP.

CIDR—see *classless interdomain routing.*

class—depending on how many bits of an IP address make up the network part, the address can be Class A, B, or C.

classless interdomain routing—a scheme for eliminating classes and dealing with networks and subnets strictly as a network address and subnet mask.

client—a computer attached to a network that uses a service.

configuration parameters—values used to initialize and configure the operating system of a computer, especially the networking part.

database—for our purposes, a way of storing data associated with a key value and retrieving it efficiently later.

datagram—a packet that contains within itself enough information for the network to deliver it to its destination.

DHCP—see *dynamic host configuration protocol.*

digital signature—the result of a cryptographic function being applied to a message; sent along with a message, it allows the recipient to verify the identity of the sender and the integrity of the message.

DNS—see *domain name system.*

domain name—the hierarchical name given to a computer on the Internet.

domain name system—the Internet system for resolving domain names to IP addresses, and vice versa.

dynamic DNS—the scheme whereby DHCP servers and clients are able to update their DNS entries as they receive new IP addresses.

dynamic host configuration protocol—the successor to BOOTP, a protocol for delivering address and configuration information to network clients.

ethernet—a network technology in wide use as a Local Area Network (LAN), invented at Xerox PARC.

ethernet address—the six-byte, globally unique address used by Ethernet.

ethertype—a field in the Ethernet header that identifies the protocol to which the rest of the frame should be delivered.

exponential backoff—increasing the retransmission time exponentially so as to avoid network congestion.

file transfer protocol—a protocol for moving files across a network.

finite state machines—for this book, a technique for designing protocols and protocol implementations.

flow—the sequence of packets that make up a network session or transaction.

FQDN—see *fully qualified domain name.*

FTP—see *file transfer protocol.*

fully-qualified domain name—a domain name with all domain parts specified, up to the root of the DNS tree.

gateway—another, older term for router.

hardware address—the address used in the physical layer of a network; the Ethernet address is an example.

hexadecimal—expressed in base 16 notation.

host—a computer attached to a network.

host byte order—the byte order used in storing information in a given computer. See also *network byte order.*

HTML—see *hypertext markup language.*

HTTP—see *hypertext transfer protocol.*

hypertext markup language—the system of formatting documents for the World Wide Web.

hypertext transfer protocol—the protocol used to transfer HTML-formatted and other documents across the World Wide Web.

IEEE—see *institute of electrical and electronics engineers, inc.*

IETF—see *internet engineering task force.*

institute of electrical and electronics engineers, inc.—international professional organization of engineers. Administers Ethernet address assignments.

internet—the global concatenation of IP-based networks.

internet draft—a working document of the IETF.

internet engineering task force—group of interested people who specify, design, implement, and argue about Internet protocols.

internic—the Internet Network Information Center, a body that administers IP address assignment or delegates portions of it to national bodies.

IP address—the 32-bit address of a host connected to the Internet. Must be globally unique.

IP—the Internet Protocol; the basic protocol of the Internet which allows hosts connected to the Internet to exchange packets. Also called IPv4.

IPv6—the "next generation" Internet protocol, successor to IPv4.

key—data used to encrypt or decrypt messages.

LDAP—see *lightweight directory access protocol.*

lease—association of a hardware address with an IP address and expiration time.

lightweight directory access protocol—the simplified version of the OSI Directory Access Protocol, standardized by the IETF and widely used to provide directory service on the Internet.

MAC address—Media Access Layer address; another term for hardware address.

MD5—a strong (today) cryptographic hash system that can be used to generate digital signatures.

network byte order—the standardized order used to send multi-byte numbers over a network. See also *host byte order.*

network information center—see *internic.*

network manager—a person who controls, manages, administers, and configures a computer network.

network segment—a piece of a network, usually not including any equipment that connects it to another piece of network. A single section of an Ethernet, for instance, or one token ring. Also called a LAN segment. Often associated with a subnet.

network—the transmission medium over which computers exchange data, together with the equipment that facilitates the exchange.

NIC—see *network information center*

octet—a data item made up of eight bits, one byte in most modern computers.

organizationally unique identifier—an identifier assigned to an organization by a standards body. A subset of OUIs is administered by the IETF; also the three-byte manufacturer portion of an Ethernet address administered by the IEEE.

OUI—see *organizationally unique identifier*.

packet—a unit of computer data that can be sent from one computer to another over a network.

padding—meaningless data appended to or inserted in a data structure so as to cause it to be a certain length or to cause data fields to align in a certain way. Good practice calls for padding to be filled with zeros.

pool—see *address pool*.

port—a 16-bit number used to identify the program or entity on a computer that produced or will consume a packet.

public-key cryptography—a cryotographic scheme in which a portion of the key is made public so as to allow one party to encrypt data only the specified other party can decrypt, without needing to exchange secret keys.

rebinding timer—the timer that tells a DHCP client when it is time to attempt to negotiate a new lease.

relay agent—an entity that forwards BOOTP and DHCP messages between a server and client on different subnets.

renewing timer—the timer that tells a DHCP client when it is time to attempt to renew its lease.

request for comments—documents published by the IETF.

resource records—data stored in the DNS.

RFC—see *request for comments*.

root servers—the well-known DNS servers at the top of the hierarchy.

rough consensus—the kind of agreement reached in IETF working groups to move documents toward standard status.

router—a machine that forwards packets from one network segment to another.

RSA data security—a cryptographic software company founded by Rivest, Shamir, and Adleman; owner of certain patented cryptographic algorithms.

schema—the way data are represented in LDAP.

scope—Windows NT term for the address pool associated with a subnet.

server—a computer attached to a network that provides a service for other computers on the network.

state machine diagrams—a graphical way of representing finite state machines.

static addresses—fixed, unchanging IP addresses delivered to special clients with DHCP.

subnet—a portion of a network with a contiguous range of IP addresses.

subnet mask—a bit mask that identifies the network part of an IP address from the host part.

superscope—Windows NT term for a concatenation of scopes, *q.v.*

T1—see *renewing timer.*

T2—see *rebinding timer.*

TCP—see *transmission control protocol.*

TFTP—see *trivial file transfer protocol.*

topology—how subnets are connected to form a network.

transmission control protocol—reliable data stream protocol widely used on the Internet.

trivial file transfer protocol—very simple but inefficient protocol usually used for loading boot files; easily included in a machine's boot ROM.

UDP—see *unreliable datagram protocol.*

uniform resource locator—string used to represent the location of an HTML document or other resource in the World Wide Web.

unreliable datagram protocol—simple protocol suitable for transmitting single messages to another computer.

URL—see *uniform resource locator.*

working groups—division of the IETF that focuses on a specific problem.

world wide web—the global collection of computers acting as HTTP servers.

WWW—see *world wide web.*

zone—portion of the DNS namespace delegated to a single DNS server, less the portions it delegates to others.

Bibliography

Albitz, Paul and Cricket Liu. *DNS and BIND*, 2nd Ed. O'Reilly & Associates, Inc. Sebastapol, CA.

Alexander, S and R. Droms. *DHCP Options and BOOTP Vendor Extensions*. RFC 2132, March 1997.

Alexander, S. and R. Droms. *DHCP Options and BOOTP Vendor Extensions*. RFC 1533, October 1993.

Croft, W.J and J. Gilmore. *Bootstrap Protocol*. RFC 951, Sep-01-1985.

Droms, R. *Dynamic Host Configuration Protocol*. RFC 2131, March 1997.

Droms, R. *Interoperation Between DHCP and BOOTP*. RFC 1534, October 1993.

Droms, R.. *Dynamic Host Configuration Protocol*. RFC 1531, October 1993.

Eastlake, D. *Secure Domain Name System Dynamic Update*. RFC 2137, April 1997.

Metcalfe, Robert M. and David R. Boggs. *Ethernet: Distributed Packet Switching for Local Computer Networks*. Xerox PARC Technical Report, November 1975; reprinted January 1976 .

Kaufman, Charlie, Radia Perlman, and Mike Speciner. *Network Security: Private Communication in a Public World*. Prentice Hall, 1995.

Prindeville, P.A. *BOOTP vendor information extensions*. RFC 1048, Feb-01-1988.

Provan, D. *DHCP Options for Novell Directory Services*. RFC 2241, November 1997.

Reynolds, J. *BOOTP Vendor Information Extensions*. RFC 1395, January 1993.

Reynolds, J. K. *BOOTP vendor information extensions*. RCF 1084, Dec-01-1988.

Vixie, P. Ed., S. Thomson, Y. Rekhter, J. Bound. *Dynamic Updates in the Domain Name System (DNS UPDATE)*. RFC 2136, April 1997.

Wimer, W. *Clarifications and Extensions for the Bootstrap Protocol*. RFC 1532, October 1993.

Wimer, W. *Clarifications and Extensions for the Bootstrap Protocol*. RFC 1542, October 1993.

Index